T M and the Nature of Enlightenment

T M

and the Nature of Enlightenment

Creative Intelligence and the
Teachings of Maharishi Mahesh Yogi

ANTHONY CAMPBELL

PERENNIAL LIBRARY
Harper & Row, Publishers
New York, Hagerstown, San Francisco, London

First PERENNIAL LIBRARY edition published 1976.

LIBRARY OF CONGRESS CATALOG CARD NUMBER: 75–29540

STANDARD BOOK NUMBER: 06–080366–5

76 77 78 79 80 10 9 8 7 6 5 4 3 2

To the many friends and meditators whose warm reception of Seven States of Consciousness *has encouraged me to write this book*

Contents

PART ONE

I

Introductory

THERE IS TODAY in the West a wave of interest in "meditation" which is probably without parallel in our history. There are wide variations, of course, in what people understand by the word, and in what they think meditation can do for them. To some, perhaps the majority, meditation suggests merely relaxation, a means of ridding oneself of some of the tensions accumulated in urban life. To others, it is concerned with self-discovery and the quest for the ultimate purpose of life. And naturally there is a wide range of attitudes between these extremes.

For most people, I imagine, the word "meditation" immediately brings to mind Maharishi Mahesh Yogi and his technique of Transcendental Meditation (TM). There are good reasons why this should be so, for although many visitors have come from the East in recent years with various techniques and philosophies, Maharishi differs from the rest in a number of important respects which have given TM an unusually wide appeal.

In the first place, Maharishi claims that TM can be taught to anyone with a reasonably intact mind and brain, that it can be easily learned and produces immediate mental and physical benefits. This sounds surprising, when one considers that nearly all teachers in the past have insisted on the great difficulty of meditation and the need for many years of practice before anything much could happen. However, Maharishi's claims about TM have now been substantiated not only by the subjective experience of hundreds of thousands of practitioners all over the world but also by scientific measurements of its physiological and psychological effects. Although these studies are still in their infancy, it is at least clear by now that *something* happens during TM. It is also clear that TM does not (except incidentally) induce sleep, nor is it a form of hypnosis. What it actually is, I shall try to show in the course of this book.

The second way in which Maharishi differs from most other exponents of Eastern philosophies is in his theoretical approach. Just as he has stood the conventional teaching on its head by insisting that meditation is easy, so he has adopted a revolutionary attitude to many of the most firmly ensconced present-day Indian beliefs about human existence and the universe. One of the most important of his innovations (or, as he would prefer to say, revivals of forgotten truths) concerns the relationship between meditation and ethics. Conventional Indian teachers insist that deeper experience in meditation comes only through "purification" by right action. For Maharishi, it is meditation which *produces* purification and so leads to right action spontaneously.

Again, there is much talk in India of renunciation, the usual implication being that the way to achieve "enlightenment" is to act as little as possible. Maharishi holds that this teaching results from confusing the way of the recluse with that of the person who is active in the world, and that this confusion is responsible for the backward condition of modern India. According to him, meditation is certainly a time for withdrawal from activity, but once that time is over activity is not merely to be tolerated but is actually the path to enlightenment.

On both the practical and the theoretical levels, then, Maharishi's teaching is of a kind which the activist Westerner finds easy to assimilate. Moreover, TM is a wholly practical technique which does not require any prior acceptance of dogma or concepts from those who want to try it. To learn TM, all that one requires is a willingness to follow simple practical instructions. It is not even necessary to believe in the effectiveness of the technique beforehand. This last idea often astonishes people, so difficult is it to rid oneself of the notion that TM *must* be some sort of self-suggestion; nevertheless it is perfectly true. A certain amount of scepticism at the outset is actually helpful, because it prevents the new meditator from looking too eagerly for results and so spoiling the naturalness of the process.

A third reason for Maharishi's success has been the enthusiasm he has shown for relating his teaching, practical and theoretical, to Western science. A number of previous Indian and Buddhist teachers have made rather vague gestures in the direction of science, but as a rule these have been unconvincing in detail, largely because the teachers in question usually knew very little about science. Maharishi has gone a good deal further. During his widespread travels in Europe and America he has seized every opportunity which has come his way to make contact with scientists, and in the last few years he has enlisted the full-time co-operation of a large number of physicists, biologists, psychologists and others who are currently helping him to relate his ideas to scientific thought. New material based on this collaboration is constantly appearing and is being used for courses currently being taught at a number of universities and other centres in America and elsewhere.

Maharishi's insistence on the interrelatedness of the spiritual and the material is one of the most remarkable and distinctive features of his approach. For Maharishi has an impeccably orthodox background in Hinduism, and can speak with authority on the Indian religious tradition, which makes his readiness to assimilate Western ideas all the more interesting. For a number of years he was the closest disciple of a renowned Indian teacher, Swami Brahmananda Sarasvati (1869–1953), who was hailed by the late President Radhakrishnan as "Vedanta Incarnate" and was by all accounts a most remarkable man. It is to his master that Maharishi invariably attributes his own inspiration. For most of his life Swami Brahmananda was a strict recluse, but for the last thirteen years or so he was prevailed upon to become Shankaracharya of Jyotir Math, in the Himalayas. (Jyotir Math is one of four monasteries, or seats of learning, founded by the original Shankara, one of the most prominent figures in the history of the Vedanta.)

After his master's death, Maharishi remained for two years in solitude and then began to teach. He inaugurated his worldwide movement on 31 December 1957, and since then the practice of TM has spread so rapidly and widely that today almost every country has at least one centre for instruction in the technique and, as I have said, hundreds of thousands of people have been taught to practise it.

Although at first sight Maharishi's readiness to associate his teaching with science may seem surprising, it is probably in large measure actually attributable to his Indian religious background. For the distinction between mind and body, which is so characteristic of the Western philosophical and religious outlook, has always been much less sharp in Indian (and Chinese) thought. It may well be, in fact, that it was just that distinction which favoured the development of scientific thought in the West; the belief that mind and matter were separate and had nothing to do with each other may have been a factor in the coming to birth of the principle of objectivity. However this may be, that rigid separation, with all its consequences for our picture of man's relation to the rest of Nature, seems to have outlived its usefulness, and to be causing a dangerous division in the modern mind.

It is a realization of this danger which in recent years has turned the eyes of many thoughtful Westerners towards the East, for in both India and China the ancient philosophers did not distinguish sharply between the spiritual and the material but rather regarded the world as a continuum, ranging from the most ethereal spirituality at one end to the most gross materiality at the other, with all possible gradations in between. This attitude affords the grounds for a reconciliation between science and what, for want of a better word, I must call mysticism. The term is a very unsatisfactory one, suggesting as it does mystification and obscurantism; except by religious writers, it is generally used to signify vague, dreamy, and unpractical ways of thinking. Let me be quite clear that in this book I am using "mysticism" in its alternative sense, to mean the quest for understanding of the nature of man and the universe through direct intuition and apprehension.

Mysticism in this second sense is by no means opposed to science. Indeed, one can go further. As Joseph Needham points out, science and mysticism are not merely mutually compatible but in their origins are intimately bound up together. Curiously, it is rationalism and not mysticism which was the enemy of early empiricism. Thus, in China the Taoists' attitude was helpful to the development of science and technology, while that of the Confucians, with their emphasis on rationalism and their lack of interest in Nature apart from human nature, was not. Nor was this true only of China; in Europe, the theologians refused to look through Galileo's telescope on the grounds that if Galileo's findings agreed with the views of Aristotle and St Thomas Aquinas there was no point in looking, while if they did not they were wrong. On the other hand, thinkers who were strongly influenced by mysticism, such as

Giordano Bruno, Kepler, and even Newton, played a key rôle in the development of science. A similar association between mysticism and early science can be found in the history of Islam.[1]

We usually think of rationalism as a progressive force, the enemy of obscurantism and superstition, and indeed so it was in Europe in the seventeenth and eighteenth centuries. But this association is by no means the rule, and indeed, as I have said, the converse would be nearer the truth. In general, there is a tendency for rationalism to harden into legalism and formalism, and then it is mysticism which acts as the revolutionary, creative force bringing about change and evolution. This is in fact what was happening in Europe during the Middle Ages, when millenarian mystical movements such as the cult of the Free Spirit arose as a reaction against the oppressive orthodoxy of the church; the Cathars (Albigensians) of southern France afford another example of the same trend.

A similar situation, I believe, has come about today. Once more, rationalism has fossilized into orthodoxy, and instinctively people are rebelling against it. That is why there are today so many manifestations of mysticism, both bad and good; and it is, I suggest, against this background that we should view the teachings of Maharishi.

The importance of this theme at the present time cannot, I think, be easily exaggerated, which is why I am returning to it so soon after writing my earlier book on TM, *Seven States of Consciousness*. Maharishi's teaching has, I am convinced, the profoundest possible relevance to the crisis through which our civilization is passing, and I should like to play a part, however small, in bringing this out.*

There is naturally an enormous number of ways in which this might be done. The approach which comes most naturally to me, and which I have followed in both books, is to try to relate various aspects of Maharishi's views to ideas in present-day science and philosophy which happen to interest me. It follows that I am not attempting to present a compendium of Maharishi's philosophy, nor do I presume to "interpret" his thought. However, having both practised and taught TM for a number of years, and having also had the privilege of listening

* See Part IV

to Maharishi and questioning him, I find that his ideas illuminate a vast range of problems and areas which were previously heavily shadowed for me, and it is this illumination which I want to convey.

At this point, it may be as well if I make clear my own attitude to Maharishi's teaching. It will by now be evident that I think TM is capable of producing far-reaching mental and physical benefits; I have in fact no doubts that it ought to be universally adopted as a means for reducing the effects of stress.

It will also be evident that I am impressed by the importance of Maharishi's philosophy, and many people who are quite willing to grant the effectiveness of TM as a technique of relaxation may find this aspect harder to accept. My own conviction, however, is that if our civilization is to survive it will have to base itself on what Aldous Huxley (who borrowed the term from Leibniz) called the Perennial Philosophy—that is, "the metaphysic which recognizes a divine Reality substantial to the world of things and lives and minds; the psychology that finds in the soul something similar to, or even identical with, divine Reality; the ethic that places man's final end in the knowledge of the immanent and transcendental Ground of all being . . . ".[2] And I believe that Maharishi has achieved a modern restatement of this timeless truth which is of the greatest possible practical significance.

Some readers may feel that, in saying this, I have marked myself out as a "believer" and hence as biased. Unfortunately, there seems no easy way out of this dilemma. If one is not oneself a practitioner of TM, one can have no first-hand knowledge of it, but if one is a practitioner one is *ipso facto* biased. Two points, however, seem worth making.

The first is that the dispassionate, objective observer does not exist; he is a fiction, an unattainable ideal, like a Euclidean point. This is true even in the exact sciences; how much more so with regard to something like TM. We are all biased, whether we recognize it or not; the decision *not* to learn TM is evidence of an attitude just as much as is the decision to do so. There are, of course, degrees of bias or open-mindedness, but that is a different matter. All that any writer can do is to declare his own position and let his readers make up their own minds about what he says. (I have given an account of my own intellectual development in the Introduction to my *Seven States of Consciousness*.)

The second point is that what Maharishi offers is not a religion or a belief system but a description of reality as seen from a particular standpoint—that of "enlightenment". To call Maharishi's teaching a philosophy would thus be somewhat misleading, for its essential underpinning is the practice of TM. How you think, and how you perceive the world, depend on your state of consciousness. While dreaming, for example, you experience quite a different world from when you are awake. A fundamental premise of Maharishi's teaching is that what we call our ordinary waking state does not exhaust all the possibilities of consciousness. There are several other states of consciousness which it is possible for us to experience. These are "normal"—unlike, say, drug-induced states—and they afford truer insights into reality than does our ordinary state. The so-called ordinary state, in fact, is actually a sub-normal condition, which bears much the same relation to the state of enlightenment as does being half-asleep to full wakefulness.

Wakefulness or the lack of it depend on the physiological condition of one's brain and body. So, too, with enlightenment; this is based on physiology. Moreover, descriptions of the nature of reality by the enlightened will have meaning for the reader only in so far as he or she is physiologically capable of understanding them. This may seem to amount only to saying that one's understanding depends on the quality of one's brain, and hence on one's intelligence, which is obvious enough. However, Maharishi's thesis is that the practice of TM actually enhances, at the physiological level, the ability of the mind to comprehend reality.

Maharishi, then, is concerned with knowledge; but knowledge in a special sense. One of the phrases he uses most frequently is "knowledge is structured in consciousness". What you know depends on the state of your mind and brain. To quote Aldous Huxley again: "Knowledge is a function of being. When there is a change in the being of the knower, there is a corresponding change in the nature and amount of knowledge."[3] This is Maharishi's position exactly.

Notice that no special claim is necessarily implied about people who practise TM. We are all in *some* state of conscious-

ness, whether we meditate or not, and a non-meditator may
well be naturally in a clearer state of awareness than someone
who has been meditating for a long time; it all depends where
you start.

The Science of Creative Intelligence (SCI)

From what I have said, it should be evident that what Maharishi
is teaching is not a religion, a philosophy, or a psychology in
the usual senses of these words, although it has elements of
them all. What, then, is it?

In recent years Maharishi has given his system the name
"Science of Creative Intelligence". He speaks of this as having
both a theoretical and a practical aspect—the practical aspect,
of course, being TM. Why "science"? Mainly, I think, because Maharishi wants to emphasize the practical and systematic nature of his teaching, and the extent to which it can
be verified experimentally. It is, of course, a "subjective"
science, for although it is quite true that the physiological and
psychological effects of TM can be studied objectively, the
changes in awareness cannot. However, I do not think that this
is a valid reason for refusing the name "science" to what
Maharishi teaches.

The West has, in fact, made at least one abortive attempt to
develop a subjective path to knowledge. At the end of the
nineteenth century there arose in Germany a "structuralist"
school of psychology, led by Wilhelm Wundt, which aimed at
achieving psychological understanding through introspection.
A psychological laboratory was set up at Leipzig in 1879, and
over the next few years similar laboratories were installed at
many other German universities and later in America, where
William James worked on experimental psychology at Harvard.
Eventually, however, the introspective method fell into dis-
repute, largely because it failed to live up to expectations. To
most modern psychologists and philosophers, the attempt to
discover truth by the subjective approach is self-evidently
absurd, and the failure of Wundt and his collaborators could
have been predicted from the start. One modern psychologist
who disagrees with this assessment, however, is John Beloff,
who thinks that the introspective method was not a wholly
mistaken enterprise, even though it failed in the end.[4] In any

case, the introspective school did produce one masterpiece: William James's monumental *Principles of Psychology*. This fascinating work ranges far beyond the boundaries of what would be called psychology today and encompasses philosophical and ethical problems; and, since it is also enlivened by James's charm and wit, it remains readable today, some 70 years after its publication—a feat which few modern textbooks of psychology seem likely to emulate.

I myself would suggest that one of the main reasons for the failure of introspection as a means to self-knowledge was that it is the wrong technique to use. But the subjective path to knowledge remains a valid one and, indeed, a necessary one to use if we are to gain a fully adequate view of human nature. Throughout the twentieth century, mainstream psychology has become increasingly objective—in fact, it has largely become the study of behaviour, and in practice this has meant principally the behaviour of the white rat. This is all very well so far as it goes; as the American psychologist H. F. Harlow has said: "I am not for one moment disparaging the value of the rat as a subject for psychological investigation; there is very little wrong with the rat that cannot be overcome by the education of the experimenters".[5] But studying rats does not tell one much about the human *psyche*.

What we really need is not rat knowledge but *self*-knowledge, and this is what SCI claims to supply. But I do not want to give the impression that SCI is a system of psychology; it is both less and more than that.

SCI is not concerned with the accumulation of facts or the construction of theories, but with the basis of all knowledge. Maharishi believes—and here, of course, he is following an ancient and widespread tradition in both East and West—that if one once understands the principles which govern one's own mind, one will also understand the principles that govern existence in general. In other words, the foundation of our minds and of the universe—of inner and outer reality—is what Maharishi calls Creative Intelligence.

The concept of Creative Intelligence is a very important one, which I shall have to use frequently and which underlies the whole argument of the book.

Creativity refers to the productiveness and variety of life, which constantly gives rise to new forms and, on the mental level, to new ideas. *Intelligence* refers to the fact that this creativity is not haphazard but takes an ordered form; atoms, for example, form crystals, cells build up into complex organisms, and so on. Taken as a whole, the phrase "Creative Intelligence" refers to that basic propensity of the universe, which we see but cannot explain, to diversify and evolve in an orderly manner.

The most characteristic feature of living organisms is that they show an apparently spontaneous tendency to produce order, to generate ever more complex patterns. (This is also true of the inanimate world in certain important respects; for example, the growth of crystals, the way in which "elementary particles" become arranged into atoms and atoms are collected into stars, galaxies, planetary systems and so on.) Today scientists of many kinds, but especially biologists, are becoming more and more preoccupied with the study of pattern. It is complexity of pattern that chiefly distinguishes living from non-living matter, and evolution is largely synonymous with the generation of order. The human brain is the supreme example of orderly complexity known to us.

The concept of order is closely related to that of purpose. One of the main reasons why Maharishi's teaching has had such a wide appeal, especially to the young, is, I believe, that it satisfies an instinctive human need to feel that there is a "purpose" to be found at work in the universe. To many people, it seems today as if science had once and for all disproved the notion of purpose. Any purpose which we think we see in Nature we read into her ourselves; it has no more existence outside our own minds than do the faces which the rain and wind sculpt in rocks.

For Maharishi, however, the very opposite is true. Human purposes reflect cosmic purposes, and are built into the very structure of the world. (To prevent misunderstanding, let me reiterate that I am not saying that Maharishi has discovered this idea for the first time—indeed, it is one of the most ancient of human ideas—but he has brought it up to date and given it a practical expression suitable for our time.)

If this idea is right, it contains the seed of a reconciliation between science and religion, and it provides a basis for what is probably the most important of all human aspirations—to feel that life makes sense. The desire to make sense of the

universe is common to both science and religion, and it is a
tragedy that they should have become divorced and mutually
opposed as they have in the West. I am sure that a reunion
between them will one day occur, because they are ultimately
engaged in the same quest for understanding; the scientist is
trying to establish through reason and experiment what the
mystic intuits directly—the Unity which underlies the manifest
plurality of the world.

There is, in fact, a common element which links a number of
key human activities, such as science, art, and metaphysics
with each other and also with mystical experience. This common element is creativity. I emphasize the fundamental
similarity of the scientific, artistic, and religious experiences because I am assuming it throughout this book even when I am
not specifically saying so. The point is important, for in spite
of C. P. Snow's lament, now some twenty years old, about the
rift between the "two cultures", there still seems to be a deep
division in many people's minds between art and science (let
alone between science and religion). I am convinced myself
that, in so far as there is a division, it reflects our failure to
comprehend the real nature of both science and art. Leonardo
da Vinci would not have seen a division, nor would the Greeks,
nor would the ancient Chinese or Indians. I like to think that
we, too, shall one day come to realize the essential unity which
underlies all forms of human creativity.

Conclusion

I hope that this preamble will lead you to approach the arguments I shall put forward in this book with some degree of
sympathy even if you do feel yourself to be biased primarily to
one or other culture. People who have little liking for science
may feel that there is too much about the brain and its workings, while some scientists may think that I have speculated too
wildly and extrapolated too far from known facts. Both criti-
cisms will no doubt have some justification. However, I am
unrepentant, for it is just the no-man's land forming a common
boundary for science, art, metaphysics, and religion which
specially fascinates me. To travel there is risky, but with a little
luck one can sometimes bring back a few interesting finds.

My plan of approach has two main elements. First, I want

to suggest a hypothesis about how TM produces its effects. Here I shall be concentrating on the individual. Second, I want to put TM in a wider context, and to look at what my hypothesis implies for Maharishi's claim that TM can solve the problems that face our society.

The book falls into four sections. Part One is introductory, and sets out the main ideas which the subsequent sections will deal with in more detail. In Part Two I put forward a view of how the brain works. I am, I hope, aware of the rashness of such an undertaking; but if one is going to discuss the mechanism of TM at all one has to have *some* picture in mind of what is happening in the brain, and I think it is best to declare one's own hand at the beginning. I have assembled my "brain model" from a wide range of components currently on display in the writings of various neuroscientists. It is only fair to warn non-scientists that this is a personal interpretation, and should not be taken as a popularization of scientific orthodoxy. It is important to say this, because all too often the unwary general reader is fobbed off with the latest hypothesis about the brain as if it were established fact, and moreover is sometimes even exhorted to adopt some ethical ,or philosophical viewpoint favoured by the writer on these "scientific" grounds. I cannot emphasize too strongly that all such arguments are tendentious and dishonest unless qualified with the reservation that their "scientific" basis is provisional. The fact is that present understanding of the brain is still embryonic, and all the really interesting questions are very far from having satisfactory answers. I believe that my own hypothesis is compatible with the known facts, and I myself find it helpful in thinking about the experience of TM; I would not claim more than that.

In Part Three I apply the brain model developed in Part Two to the experience of TM. Part Four is the most speculative and ambitious section of the book, for here I try to apply the concepts I have used to the problems which confront us as a society, and try to show what, in my view, is the real significance of Maharishi's teaching. This, no doubt, is an even more rash undertaking than that of Part Two, yet I think it needs to be made since the ultimate justification of TM is the effects it is claimed to have on society.

The various sections of the book are interdependent, but there is no reason why anyone who finds one hard going should

not skip. This particularly applies to Part Two, which is un-
avoidably somewhat technical, though I have tried to make it
as readable and self-explanatory as possible.

Acknowledgements

It remains only to express my gratitude and indebtedness
to all those on whose thoughts and creativity I have drawn in
writing. My chief debt, naturally, is to Maharishi himself,
both for the technique of TM itself and for its underlying
philosophy. Without him, obviously, there would have been
no book.

At a different level, my debt to a number of contemporary
scientists and thinkers will be evident in what follows. I am
specially grateful to Gregory Bateson, whose drawing out of the
implications of cybernetics supplied me with many of my basic
ideas; to Professor Karl Pribram, on whose theories about the
brain I have leaned heavily; and (in Part Two) to Professor
Joseph Needham, whose monumental *Science and Civilization
in China* provided me with a host of new ways of looking at
SCI in historical terms. The chapter notes will make clear
how far I have drawn upon these authorities and others, but
it need hardly be said that they must not be held responsible
for the use I have made of their ideas. This particularly applies
to Pribram, whose cybernetic model I have extended a good
deal further than there is warrant for in his writings. But—
to borrow a phrase from Miller, Galanter and Pribram—my
only hope is that there is such a thing as creative misunderstanding.

TM and the Evolution of Consciousness

IN PART ONE my main aim will be to discuss the experience of TM in relation to what is currently known about the brain. To do this, I shall have to refer frequently to various aspects of the TM experience, and so if you are not yet yourself practising TM you will need a general idea of what it is. I think it is best to set this out as plainly as possible in the beginning of the book; meditators may prefer to skip this chapter, but non-meditators will, I think, find that it provides a necessary frame of reference. To prevent misunderstanding, however, I must make it clear that I can give the principle only here; the actual technique is always taught personally. This is not out of any desire on Maharishi's part for mystification, but is an inevitable consequence of the fact that experience during TM occurs along a dimension of the mind which we do not usually explore. As soon as one begins to meditate, one finds oneself in a different phase of experience, and unless one has a guide one will not be able to understand what is happening.

This is not because the experiences will necessarily be bizarre or extraordinary—indeed, they may well be just the opposite, in which case it is their ordinariness that will need to be explained. The point is, however, that it would be quite impractical to describe in advance all the possible experiences which could occur, and moreover to do so would spoil their spontaneity and might lead people merely to imagine the experiences instead of coming to them "innocently". (Notice, incidentally, how this feature of TM marks it off from hypnosis, in which every effort is made to increase the power of suggestion to the maximum.)

What, then, is TM?

I think the best way of answering this question is to quote what Maharishi himself has said about TM and then enlarge upon it. Maharishi's own description of TM runs as follows.

The technique may be defined as turning the attention inwards towards the subtler levels of a thought until the mind transcends the experience of the subtlest state of the thought and arrives at the source of the thought. This expands the conscious mind and at the same time brings it in contact with the creative intelligence that gives rise to every thought.

A thought-impulse starts from the silent creative centre within, as a bubble starts from the bottom of the sea. As it rises, it becomes larger; arriving at the conscious level of the mind, it becomes large enough to be appreciated as a thought, and from there it develops into speech and action.[1]

Now, the first thing to notice about this is the implied model of the mind, which is that of the sea. The mind, in other words, is thought of as having depth.* Meditation consists in shifting the attention from the surface to the deeper layers, and ultimately to the sea bottom. Maharishi, in fact, often speaks of TM as being like diving, while ordinary thinking is like swimming on the surface.

At this point I need to introduce two important technical terms. Movement "downwards" is described as movement in the direction of increasing *subtlety*, whereas movement in the opposite direction—towards the surface—is towards increasing *grossness*. (See fig. 1.) It follows that one can experience a large number of different grades of thought, from the grossest level, at the surface of the mind, to the subtlest, next to the sea

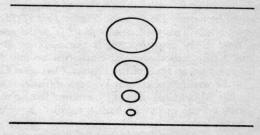

FIGURE I

* It is best not to try to relate this model to Jungian or other psychoanalytic "depth" models of the mind, because although resemblances do exist there are also important differences.

bottom. It is essential to understand that the concept of subtlety has nothing to do with the *content* of the thought, but only with its quality. To describe the quality of subtlety in words is almost impossible, partly for the reason that subtle thought is not verbal. As I shall show in later chapters, subtle thought is the kind associated with creativity. Probably everyone experiences it to some degree, although some do so more than others. One form of subtle thought is the kind which flits through the mind and is gone almost before one is aware of it, but this is still at a comparatively gross level and there are many layers of even subtler thought below which are not accessible except through transcending. (The word "transcending", which is used here simply in the sense of "going beyond", refers to the experiencing of these subtler layers of thought.)

So far, perhaps, nothing I have said about TM marks it out clearly from other systems of meditation currently being taught. What is unique (so far as I know) about TM, however, is Maharishi's claim that it is easy, natural, and effortless. To anyone who has done any reading about meditation before encountering Maharishi's ideas—and still more to anyone who has actually practised another technique—Maharishi's claim is likely to sound astonishing and almost incredible. The orthodox teaching today is that meditation requires near-superhuman efforts at concentration, the aim being to "exclude thoughts" and "make the mind a blank".

Traces of a different understanding current in earlier times are in fact to be found. Thus, in the *Tibetan Book of The Great Liberation* we read "This meditation, *devoid of mental concentration*, free from every imperfection, is the most excellent of meditations"[2] [my italics]. Similar hints can be found elsewhere: for example, in texts of the Eastern Orthodox Church and also in the writings of certain Western spiritual teachers, such as the late Abbot Chapman of Downside.[3] But, in modern times at least, no one except Maharishi seems to have understood the secret fully.

The essence of Maharishi's insight is, like many ideas of genius, very simple once it has been grasped. It is based on two principles.

1. *Experience of one's inner nature yields supreme happiness.* All the religious and philosophical traditions, both Eastern and

Western, which have described this experience agree that it has, in fact, this characteristic—the Vedantists speak of "bliss consciousness", and the Gospels of the kingdom of God within—but it is the stripping away of the outer layers of the personality which is usually represented as immensely difficult. At this point, however, we encounter Maharishi's second principle.

2. *The mind naturally seeks for happiness.* This, of course, is a near-truism. Every living creature, from amoeba to man, seeks the things it likes or needs and avoids those it dislikes or which threaten it. Putting these two ideas together, we reach the apparently obvious, but none the less revolutionary, conclusion that *movement towards increasing levels of subtlety ought to be natural and effortless.*

At any point in the mind-ocean, the layer of experience immediately beneath the one where you happen to be will be more attractive, and hence will pull the attention "downwards". Hence movement downwards is natural, and the attention sinks towards the bottom of the mind as if it were a stone.

In the ordinary way, our attention is directed outwards, through the senses. If, however, one turns it inwards, it will automatically be drawn further and further onwards, as a moth is drawn towards a light. Perhaps I may anticipate one of my main themes in this book by pointing out that this is a very cybernetic idea; movement towards subtler layers of the mind occurs through a process of positive feedback, in which each step nearer the goal is confirmed by an experience of increased happiness.

In practical terms, one needs a particular thought to experience in its subtler and subtler aspects. For this purpose a special sound, or *mantra*, is used. *When correctly employed* (and this is where personal instruction is so vital), the mantra *spontaneously* is experienced at subtler and subtler levels of the mind. Eventually, when it has reached the ultimate degree of subtlety, it disappears altogether, leaving the meditator awake but with nothing to experience. (In terms of the sea analogy, he is now on the sea bed.) At this point, thinking has been transcended, and has therefore ceased, but this is quite different from "making the mind a blank". I will return to this point shortly.

The mantra in TM serves much the same purpose that a heavy stone does to a pearl fisherman; it helps with the dive.

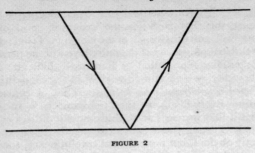

In addition, however, it is supposed to exert a "refining" influence on the nervous system. Notice that it is the vibrational effects of the mantra, rather than any meaning it may possess, which is important. Maharishi has defined a mantra as a sound whose effects are known. To some Westerners, the idea smacks of magic and mumbo jumbo, but this is to misunderstand the underlying principle. The mantra could be thought of as a template, or seed crystal, which gives a pattern to the psychophysical structure. It is an organizing element; it supplies a pattern.

The clue to understanding how TM works is to realize that it is the very opposite of concentration and effort; it is expansion, letting go. TM is concerned with freedom. In many Indian texts one finds the mind compared to a monkey, aimlessly jumping from branch to branch. The task of the meditator is said to be to catch the monkey and restrain it forcibly. Maharishi's technique is entirely different: instead of trying to restrain the monkey, put out some of its favourite food and it will always be found where one wants it. Maharishi often compares the mind, not to a monkey, but to a honey bee, which certainly flies from flower to flower but always in search of the finest nectar which, if it finds, it will not leave.

TM is in fact a kind of mental judo. Instead of trying to overcome the natural tendency of the mind to wander, TM makes use of it by letting the mind wander freely in the direction of increasing happiness.

It is the utter simplicity and, indeed—once one has been shown it—obviousness of Maharishi's insight that is at once the strength and weakness of TM: strength, because it works;

weakness, because people find it hard to believe that anything so effortless should be so effective. Especially if one has spent years in attempting to control the mind, it seems almost incredible that the secret of meditation should consist in doing the very opposite.

It seems to be this astonishing simplicity which has caused the secret of meditation to be lost so often in the past. Human beings have an incurable tendency to make straightforward things complicated, and, in the case of TM, once this is done— once one tries to "help" the process by making any sort of effort—nothing happens at all. The natural response is to try harder, and the more one tries the less happens. Then all sorts of rationalizations are introduced to explain the need for still greater efforts: one must give up the lesser good for the sake of the greater, and so on. But all these arguments are beside the point if meditation is, in fact, simple—and the experience of many thousands of practitioners of TM has by now shown that it is.

The TM Experience

At this point, I should like to offer a description of a "typical" meditation period. I have put "typical" in quotation marks because there is really no such thing as a typical meditation period. The widest possible variations may occur from person to person, and, indeed, from time to time in the case of the same person, and all these variations will be satisfactory meditation. (Hence, once again, the need for a trained teacher.) For purposes of discussion, however, I need to abstract from this wide range of possibilities a theoretical norm. Provided it is realized that my description is purely diagrammatic, no harm will be done.

TM is usually practised twice a day for fifteen or twenty minutes on each occasion. During meditation, the meditator is sitting comfortably, with closed eyes, experiencing subtler stages of thought in the manner I have described.

As the process gets under way, the attention begins to "sink". In some cases the dive may take the meditator all the way to the sea bed. More often, however, the descent occurs in a stepwise fashion. During a typical meditation period several dives occur, each one going a little deeper than its predecessor and starting from a slightly lower "platform". The result is that during the meditation period the quality of thought tends to change from gross to subtle and back again, to give a sequence of events something like that depicted in fig. 3.

I want to emphasize this wave-like character of the TM experience (always with the proviso that it is a generalization, and individual meditation periods may well be entirely different), because it provides, I believe, a very important clue to the way TM works in terms of brain function. Moreover, as I shall also explain, there are interesting correspondences between this pattern and the processes of thinking and creativity.

In Maharishi's description of TM which I quoted earlier, we found the claim that TM "expands the conscious mind".

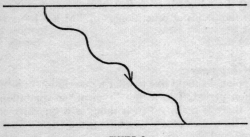

FIGURE 3

There are two ways of looking at this idea. In the first place, constant repetition of the experience of transcending day after day eventually familiarizes the meditator with the various deeper layers of the mind and so begins to make them available for conscious use. In this sense travel "inwards" expands the mind more surely and effectively than does geographical travel. There is, however, another sense in which TM expands the mind. To explain this, I must return to a point which I made a little earlier.

You will remember that I described the attention as sinking down through ever subtler regions of the mind until at last it reached the subtlest of all, just above the sea bed, and then went beyond, to the bed itself. This is the final stage in the transcending process, and—according to Maharishi—it "brings [the conscious mind] into contact with the creative intelligence that gives rise to every thought".[4] I need to look at this idea in a little more detail.

To picture what is happening at this point in meditation, we need to use a different image of the mind. Imagine that you are looking at a pool of water which is filled with ripples. Gradually these die away, becoming finer and finer (subtler and subtler) until the pool is completely still. This is an analogy for the transcending process. The activity of the mind becomes less and less, until finally it ceases altogether. This is the point where the mantra has refined itself away entirely, like the Cheshire cat, and what is left is awareness itself, like the cat's grin. This is the state which the *Bhagavad Gita* describes so beautifully as "a lamp which does not flicker in a windless place". It can be called the state of "pure awareness"—pure in the sense that there is no object of awareness, but simply awareness itself. It can also be called Self-awareness, because pure awareness is found to be the underlying reality of the mind. The Self is the boundless ocean; the ordinary mind (self) is derived from the unlimited Self by limitation. Hence, gaining Self-awareness is a process of expansion. The Self is "realized" when the activity of the mind (self) is allowed to die away. The return from the Self to the self—from pure unbounded awareness to everyday consciousness—occurs quite simply by a contrary process: pure awareness *becomes* the individual mind simply by beginning to "ripple". (Maharishi has defined mind as vibrating consciousness.)

If this analogy is accepted as a valid description of transcending, it becomes clear why concentration and effort during meditation are not merely useless but actually lead in the wrong direction. The Self is *expanded* mind, so what is the use of concentration? Similarly, the Self is realized through gaining stillness, but effort implies activity, stirring up.

From what I have just said, it will be clear that one way of describing TM would be as a technique for Self-realization. But it is important to understand that Self-realization is not in itself full enlightenment; it is only a stage on the path. I will return to this shortly, but first I want to look at TM from a different standpoint—as a physiological technique.

TM as a Physiological Technique

The physiological aspects of enlightenment do not usually receive much attention in discussions of meditation, but for Maharishi they have the greatest importance.

During TM, as the various physiological studies so far carried out have indicated, there is a reduction in many aspects of body activity; breathing rate and volume, heart output, and muscular tone all decrease, and there is a general tendency towards physical stillness. The TM state thus has some physiological resemblances to deep sleep, and people who look on TM primarily as a means of relaxation are right so far as they go.

This way of looking at the matter has led Maharishi to formulate the important concept of "stress". Again, this is something I shall have much more to say about later, but at this stage we need to have a general idea of what it means.

Throughout our waking lives, each of us is exposed to a constant bombardment of impressions. The task of the brain is to process these impressions—either to act on them immediately, or else to store them away for future reference. Sometimes, however, the impressions are too many or too strong for the system to cope with, and then it becomes overloaded. Notice that it is not only unpleasant events which can cause this overloading; joyful ones can do so too. For example, it was recently reported in a medical journal that a man in his eighties was reunited with a long-lost son whom he believed to be dead; so great was the unfortunate father's excitement that he collapsed and died—and the son promptly followed his example.

Maharishi has postulated that, whenever an impression of any kind overloads the nervous system, a lasting area of disturbance is left, and this constitutes a stress.* Notice particularly that stress has both physiological and psychological aspects. Physically, as I have said, a stress is thought of as an area of dysfunction within the brain; psychologically, it is the source of anxieties, obsessions, and other symptoms, including

* Strictly speaking, stress should be used for the environmental factor, and strain for the effects on the individual of such stress. However, it has become customary among practitioners of TM to use stress to refer to both the cause and its effects, and to avoid confusion I shall follow that usage here.

various psychosomatic ones. Most modern psychologists hold that there must be *some* physiological basis for every kind of mental disturbance, even though our present techniques are too insensitive to detect them; Maharishi holds precisely the same view.

One way in which stresses are removed is, presumably, sleep. Another is TM. Maharishi claims that there are certain kinds of stress which cannot be removed by sleep but require the more profound kind of rest supplied by TM. From the physiological point of view, then, TM is a means of ridding the nervous system of stress.

It is reasonable to expect that stress release would be a cyclical, rhythmic process, for rhythm is a basic feature of life. Every creature, every organ, and every cell seems to have its alternate periods of rest and activity. Animals and plants develop, grow old, and die, and even the universe, at least according to one currently popular cosmological model, alternately expands and contracts in a giant diastole and systole. In our own lives, one of the most familiar and fundamental of all rhythms is that of sleep and wakefulness, and although the mechanism which controls this is not understood, it seems likely that there are specific areas of the brain stem which are responsible for the rhythm.

Now, although it is still too early to be dogmatic, it seems quite likely that the pattern of alternating TM and activity into which the human system falls with such apparent ease and naturalness is a rhythm of the same general kind. If so, the failure of most of us to allow this alternation to occur would be a most important cause of the accumulation of fatigue and stress, and TM would be as necessary for efficient mental and physical activity as sleep. Maharishi certainly believes that this is the case; it is a point to which I shall return in much more detail later.

For the present, the point which I want to bring out is that the return to the surface after a dive is automatic and inevitable, *and occurs for physiological reasons*. Surfacing is as natural as diving, and is part of the same rhythmic process.

Here we have the solution to a problem which may have been puzzling you, namely, why—if the experience of subtle layers of the mind is so attractive—does the attention ever return to the surface? Why do meditators ever come out of meditation? The answer seems to be, quite simply, that people come out of meditation for much the same reason as they wake up in the morning—because their brains are so constructed that they should. The general slowing down of metabolic processes which occurs during TM represents one extreme of the pendulum swing. The system slows down, reaches a condition of maximum rest, and then returns to normal activity. TM, in fact, is a thoroughly "natural" process.

From a physiological point of view, the purpose of TM can be described as the removal of stress. But it is essential to understand that this definition in no way conflicts with the definition of TM as a means to attaining enlightenment; these are alternative ways of saying the same thing. From the psychological point of view, stress may be thought of as so many blocks within the nervous system, which interfere with clear perception and effective action. If one thinks of enlightenment as meaning, literally, the letting in of light, TM can be regarded as increasing the amount of light admitted by clearing away the obstructions (stresses) which block its path. One could roughly say that the extent of a person's enlightenment is inversely proportional to the amount of stress remaining within his system; the less the stress, the more the enlightenment.

An important implication of this is that all the higher states of consciousness which Maharishi describes—and to which I shall come in a moment—are not to be thought of as in any way strange or abnormal, but are perfectly natural results of making the system stress-free. Enlightenment is the natural human condition, and it is ignorance, the absence of enlightenment, which is abnormal.

Stress release is the explanation for the cyclical or oscillatory character of the TM experience. During the descent phase of the cycle, brain activity is decreasing; at the bottom of the trough stress is released and this release causes the activity of the brain to increase somewhat, though probably not to its original level. Once more activity begins to decrease, attention sinks, and the cycle repeats itself.

Until a given stress has been dissolved, the attention cannot sink past that point—or, to put the matter differently, no deeper experience is possible until the activity of the brain has died down. Thus the subtlety of thought at any given moment during meditation is a reflection of how much activity is going on in the nervous system—the less the activity, the more subtle the thought.

In the state of pure awareness, as I have explained, thought has ceased flickering and the mind has become quite still. There must presumably be some particular brain state corresponding to this mental state; Maharishi has called the brain state in question "restful alertness". Restful alertness is a state in which the nervous system is in some sense still, but Maharishi sharply distinguishes this state from that of deep sleep. The essential characteristic of restful alertness is that it is a condition of maximum potential energy; the brain and mind are pictured as poised for action, like a runner at the start of a race. Once thinking (activity) resumes, the potential energy of restful alertness is transformed into kinetic energy.

The Purpose of TM—Enlightenment

The purpose of practising TM is the gaining of enlightenment. We have already met this idea, when we saw that enlightenment was the state which resulted from the removal of all stress from the nervous system. Now it is time to look at the matter in more detail.

What psychological experience occurs when all stress has been released? The answer, according to Maharishi, is *permanent* Self-awareness.

At first, the state of pure awareness is entirely separate from outer experience. Indeed, the two seem to be mutually incompatible; either one is lost in meditation, or one is active. After a time, however, something of inner pure awareness begins to spill over into ordinary life, persisting even when meditation is over. In the beginning the effect is brief and slight, but as time goes on it lasts longer and becomes stronger, until eventually it becomes permanent and a condition of *dual awareness* ensues. Self-awareness now persists at all times, in whatever condition—waking, dreaming, or deep sleep—the meditator may chance to be.

This undoubtedly sounds very strange, as Maharishi himself recognizes: "If we try to render the state into words we find ourselves descending into absurdity".[5] Nevertheless it is, he insists, a psychological reality. Moreover, he also insists that it must have some physiological basis; there must be some condition of the brain which corresponds to this dual experience.

What that brain state may be it will be an important part of my task in Part Three to discuss. At present, I want to try to answer a different question, namely, what is the *use* of gaining this strange-sounding state?

To answer this fully—even if I were capable of doing so—would require a book in itself. But perhaps it will be enough for the moment if I say that the value of attaining permanent contact with this deepest layer of the mind is that it is the fountainhead of all our thoughts, and hence of our actions, and so to base oneself on that immeasurably enhances the effectiveness of everything one does. TM, in other words, is not an end in itself but is practised for the sake of its effects on everyday life.

The real purpose of TM is not to provide pleasant experiences but to bring us into contact with that layer of existence which Maharishi calls the field of Creative Intelligence. For it is from here, he insists, that we draw all our thoughts and ideas and, indeed, our very being. The solution to all the problems of life can be found only in creative thinking; new plans, new approaches are continually needed if we are to adapt and evolve, and these must come from this deepest layer of the mind. For Maharishi, the concept of a field of Creative Intelligence which can be contacted is no vague piece of metaphysics; he intends it as literal truth, and insists that the validity of his claim can be verified experimentally, through the practice of TM.

It really is impossible to over-emphasize the importance of the rôle of activity in Maharishi's philosophy. The idea of meditation is often somewhat suspect in the activist West; it tends to call up associations of passivity and withdrawal from life, and, in an extreme form, it suggests the doctrine that the world is unreal and hence of no account.

Maharishi is most emphatic that this conception of meditation is a total misunderstanding. It is to this misunderstanding that he attributes the backward condition of modern India. The only reason for meditating, he insists, is to enhance the effectiveness of action. A favourite analogy of his is shooting with a bow and arrow; to shoot a long way, one must pull the arrow back far on the bow. But one must also release it. The point is that neither pulling back nor letting go make any sense by themselves, but only as part of a sequence. So with TM: rest makes sense only in relation to subsequent activity.

Indeed, the point should be put more strongly still. It is precisely by losing pure awareness in activity that it is eventually made permanent. It is all very well to attain inner tranquillity during meditation, but what about afterwards? The tranquillity must be tempered in the fire of activity before it can be called truly established. (One must lose one's life to find it.) To illustrate this idea, Maharishi often uses the analogy of dyeing. In rural India, when cloth was to be dyed with the old vegetable dyes it was dipped in the dye and then exposed to the sun, which caused it to fade; then it was dipped again in the dye, and so on. At last there came a time when the dye no longer faded in the sun; it had become fast. In the same way, Maharishi believes, activity plays an essential part in stabilizing the fruits of meditation.

Here we encounter another seemingly revolutionary idea, and yet, like the teaching that Self-realization does not depend on effort, it may well be that the current Indian emphasis on withdrawal from activity as the only path to enlightenment is a misunderstanding. Certainly the great mystics of both East and West have been remarkable for their energy and activity. What has happened in India in the last few hundred years seems to have been confusion between the path of the recluse and that of the person who is active in the world. For the recluse it is right to withdraw from ordinary activity as much as possible (although even the recluse cannot avoid it altogether, as the *Bhagavad Gita* makes plain), but for those of us who are in the world the path to enlightenment is through activity.

Higher States of Consciousness

So far we have encountered two states of consciousness which might be called "higher". The first is pure Self-awareness. This is sometimes called the fourth state, because it is additional to the three ordinary states of waking, dreaming, and deep sleep, and also because it is the underlying reality of these three. That is to say, waking, dreaming, and deep sleep are modifications of the essential ground state of pure awareness.

Pure awareness is like a cinema screen, on which the projector
casts the images of the successive waking, dreaming, and deep
sleep states. When all these images have been removed, what is
left is the screen itself—pure awareness.

Experience of pure awareness in the fourth state is temporary,
being achieved only during meditation. *Permanent* pure awareness—maintenance of Self-awareness together with the waking,
dreaming, and deep sleep states—constitutes the fifth state.
Physiologically, this is a condition in which all blocks to
thought and action have been removed, and the system is
functioning at full efficiency.

Establishment of the fifth state is, according to Maharishi,
a necessary preliminary to the full development of the remaining higher states. It may seem a little surprising that any such
development could occur; it might be thought that permanent
Self-awareness was the ultimate which could be attained.
However, Maharishi does describe a further series of refinements which are possible.

It is perfectly true that the fifth state represents the full
flowering of inner awareness. Progress after this point depends
on modification of the mechanism of perception—that is, it is
concerned with the way the world is seen.

I do not intend to say a great deal about these higher states
here; clearly it is very difficult for someone like myself, who is
very far from first-hand experience of them, to do so. I have
gone as far in that direction as I feel I can in my earlier book
Seven States of Consciousness. In general terms, however, what
happens is that refinement of the mechanisms of sensory
perception allows the subtler values of perceived objects to
come into awareness. Let me elaborate on this for a moment.

The essence of TM, we have seen, is that it is a technique
for systematically bringing subtler aspects of the inner, mental
world into awareness. This process reaches its logical culmination in the permanent establishment of inner pure awareness.
After this point, the same process is repeated in terms of the
outer world. At first this leads to a state in which the world
is found to have become transformed and alive. Maharishi
has compared this state (the sixth) to seeing the world through
golden glasses, whereas in the fifth it is still seen through ordinary glasses. (This should not be taken to mean that the sixth
state is one of illusion; on the contrary, the golden glasses

reveal facets of the world which were always there but were previously unnoticed.)

Even the sixth state is not one of full enlightenment. This comes only in the seventh* state, in which the very subtlest values of the objects of sense are transcended and the Self, which has already been found to be the inner reality, is discovered to be the underlying outer reality also. The *Bhagavad Gita* describes this state as follows: "In a Brahmin endowed with learning and humility, in a cow, in an elephant, in a dog and even in one who has lost his caste, the enlightened perceive the same." (V, 18)[6] On this verse Maharishi makes the following comment:

> This does not mean that such a man fails to see a cow or is unable to distinguish it from a dog. Certainly he sees a cow as a cow and a dog as a dog, but the form of the cow and the form of the dog fail to blind him to the oneness of the Self, which is the same in both ... The enlightened man, while beholding and acting in the whole of diversified creation, does not fall from his steadfast Unity of life, with which his mind is saturated and which remains indelibly infused in his vision.[7]

All the higher states which I have mentioned are of the kind which is usually called mystical, although, as I have said, Maharishi dislikes the word. "Philosophers call this a mystical experience, but it is no more mysterious than is the working of a clock for a child. On one level of consciousness it is normal, on another it is mysterious, and again on another it is impossible."[8]

As I say, I shall not be much concerned in this book with any states beyond the fifth, and I mention the others only for the sake of completeness. In any case, it must be understood that the classification of the process of gaining enlightenment into different stages is largely a theoretical convenience, adopted for

---

* Quite recently Maharishi has refined his account of the higher states of consciousness by including another; this might be called an eighth state, or alternatively one could say that he has subdivided the seventh into two parts. These refinements are not important for my present purpose since I shall be concerned more with immediate practicalities.

teaching purposes. In practice, there is a good deal of over-lapping among the various stages, so that flashes of a higher state may occur long before it is fully established. Indeed, the brief spontaneous mystical or ecstatic experiences which occur to many people perhaps once or twice in a lifetime are brief episodes of higher states. For the most part, my discussion will be concerned with the mechanism of TM and stress release, since these, after all, are what concern most of us here and now; moreover they are open to direct experimentation, both subjective and objective. I do believe, however, that the argument I shall put forward has relevance to all the higher states of consciousness, and in Chapter Seven I shall suggest how it might be applied to them.

III

Himalayan Interlude

BEFORE WE PLUNGE into the main argument of the book, I think it may help to give a sense of perspective if I say a little about how I came to look at TM in the way I shall be describing.

The seed of the idea was sown in my mind by a talk given by Dr L. G. C. E. Pugh, of the Medical Research Council, at a symposium on SCI held in Birmingham in 1971.[1] Although Dr Pugh's talk did not deal with TM directly, it struck me at the time as having the greatest possible indirect relevance, and subsequently I have become increasingly convinced about this.

In January 1961 Dr Pugh was a member of an expedition to the Himalayas. To the expedition base camp at Mingbo, which is at a height of 15,300 feet, came a thirty-five-year-old pilgrim called Man Bahadur. Although the air temperature was already below freezing point, Man Bahadur wore only thin cotton trousers and jacket, a thin woollen vest, a cotton shirt, a thin woollen sleeveless pullover, an old khaki overcoat, and a large turban; he had no shoes or gloves.

Man Bahadur told the expedition that he was making a pilgrimage to the snows and would like to stay with them for a month. Concerned for his safety, Dr Pugh and his companions told him to go down to their storehouse for shelter, but he refused and spent the night with the Sherpa porters. Over the next four days he was seen on the Mingbo glacier at heights between 16,500 and 17,500 feet. On the fourth night there was a blizzard, and next day a search party was sent to look for him. He was found, alive and well, beside the river, 600 feet below the expedition camp.

During the nights Man Bahadur had spent on the glacier the temperature had fallen to between −13 and −15 degrees centigrade. Man Bahadur had had no food during this time, and had slept in the lee of a rock, covered by his overcoat. He had, he said, slept soundly and had not been awakened by shivering.

So impressed were the Sherpas by this performance that they ceased to object to Man Bahadur's presence (they had earlier taken him for a Chinese spy), and he stayed at the base camp for two weeks, where he allowed Dr Pugh to carry out physiological studies.

Among this pilgrim's minor peculiarities was a taste for glass, especially microscope slides, which he chewed up and swallowed, apparently without ill-effects. However, Dr Pugh's attention was chiefly directed towards Man Bahadur's extraordinary resistance to cold. The Sherpas, who are themselves very resistant to cold, thought it impossible that anyone could have survived the four nights which this man had spent on the glacier; and Dr Pugh knows of no case in which a climber escaped frostbite after being caught at night without protective equipment. The question is, then, how did Man Bahadur do it?

Theoretically, he had two courses open to him. He could increase his heat production, or he could reduce his heat loss. (He could also, of course, do both together, and this is what in fact he did.)

He was a thin man, so body fat was not a factor in his resistance. His clothing was remarkably thin, and afforded little protection. Some reduction in heat loss can be achieved by curling up and reducing surface area, and this Man Bahadur did at night, sleeping under the lee of a rock and covering himself with his overcoat.

Man Bahadur's chief adaptation to cold, however, was his ability to increase heat production economically. When ordinary people are exposed to cold, they respond by intermittent bouts of shivering which interfere with sleep and quickly prove exhausting. Man Bahadur, on the other hand, responded to just the right extent—not too little, not too much. He showed little tendency to shiver, and when he did shiver it was moderately and continuously, without discomfort. By shivering in this way he could raise his metabolic rate (and hence his heat production) to almost three times the expected level.

Shivering is a short-term response to cold. There is also a long-term response, which depends primarily on increasing the output of certain hormones, especially thyroid hormone, which acts as an accelerator of metabolism. (The more thyroid hormone there is in the blood, the faster the cells burn up their fuel and the more heat is produced.) When Man Bahadur was sitting quietly without shivering his metabolic rate was still 35 per cent above the expected level. (There is no direct evidence that Man Bahadur had increased his production of thyroid hormone, but it seems very likely that he had.)

Now, the point I want to emphasize is that Man Bahadur's short-term and long-term responses to cold were both *very finely adjusted*. They were nicely calculated to produce an adequate, but not a wasteful, supply of heat. Man Bahadur's whole pattern of cold adaptation provides, in fact, a beautiful example of what I shall call the *principle of fine adjustment*. Let us look at another illustration of it; this concerns control of the local temperature of the body, such as the hands and feet.

Local heat control depends on blood flow. If the blood vessels going to the part dilate, more blood flows to the surface and the skin temperature rises; if they constrict, the temperature falls. However, the situation is more complicated than this description implies.

If the blood vessels constrict too much for too long, the tissues, deprived of oxygen, will die—this is frostbite. On the other hand, if too much blood flows into the skin, heat will be wasted. Moreover, if the temperature of the feet rises too high in someone who is walking on snow, the snow melts, which is a disadvantage because snow is a much better insulator than water; once again, frostbite may result.

Man Bahadur's response took account of all this. After he had been walking barefoot on snow at −6 degrees centigrade for half an hour, the temperature of his feet was still eight degrees. The blood flow to his feet, therefore, was very finely adjusted; his feet remained warm, but not too warm.

Dr Pugh does not know how exactly Man Bahadur attained his remarkable degree of adaptation to cold. It may be that he had some yogic technique of his own; I am thinking here of the remarkable Tibetan practice of *tumo*, in which elaborate techniques involving the visualization of internal fire were apparently used to increase the heat-generating capacity of the body. Adepts used to engage in competitions, sitting naked beside mountain streams while cloths were soaked in the icy water and draped about them; the winner was he (or she) who could dry most cloths.[2]

Whether Man Bahadur had any such technique is uncertain.

He came from a village where the winter temperatures are often below freezing and the inhabitants wear clothes giving little protection and live in houses with unglazed windows. He was thus probably fairly well acclimatized to cold to start with, and would have become further acclimatized during the three-week journey to the base camp.

Whatever the true explanation may have been, however, his story is fascinating. It is not without precedent. Eskimos have the ability to keep warm without bouts of wasteful shivering. Australian aborigines can control their blood flow very precisely from area to area, so that the radial artery of the hand nearer to the fire may be constricted while that of the other hand is allowing full circulation.[3]

Animals, too, have similar mechanisms. The feet of gulls, for example, emit only a small amount of heat in cold water, and they prevent their feet from freezing by accurately registering, and responding to, very small and rapid changes in temperature in localized areas—that is, by the principle of fine adjustment.[4]

Animals and human beings use the same principle of fine adjustment to deal with the converse situation, extreme heat. Camels and other large mammals that live in the desert have developed all kinds of mechanisms and behaviour for regulating their temperature and conserving water. When human beings first go from a temperate to a tropical climate, they sweat excessively and lose much salt in their sweat, but when they have become acclimatized they sweat only just enough to control their temperature; also, the salt content of their sweat falls and so their salt stores are not depleted. Fine adjustment therefore is a widespread and vital feature of adaptation to cold.

However, it may not be immediately obvious why I found the story of Man Bahadur so exciting and important. After all, Man Bahadur was not himself practising TM, and although it may well be true that TM alters people's resistance to cold, I know of no evidence to suggest it. But what Dr Pugh's talk did for me was to focus my thoughts on the *principle* of fine adjustment, and as I thought about it I began to see that one could extend the idea far beyond the mere regulation of temperature, and that it seemed to have a great deal of relevance to TM.

I had for some time been aware from my own experience—
and had frequently confirmed it from that of other meditators—
that TM tends to produce a particular psychological effect
that sounds paradoxical when one tries to put it into words.
The best way I can describe it is to say that TM makes one *feel*
things more but be *pushed off balance* by them less.

As I say, this sounds paradoxical—but surely it corresponds
very well with the principle of fine adjustment? What Man
Bahadur, the gulls, the Eskimos and the rest were doing was to
respond precisely to the right extent; but the ability to do this
depended on accurate perception. Man Bahadur was not *insensitive*
to cold—if he had been, he would have got frostbite; he was
resistant to it, which is quite different. Before he could respond
to the cold, he had to be able to feel it, in the sense of registering
it. But he was not distressed by the cold, because he could adjust
to it by increasing his heat production.

The same idea, I believe, can be applied to the behaviour of
people who practise TM. One is sometimes asked whether
TM makes people insensitive and withdrawn. So far as I can
judge it does the exact opposite. Meditators become more
sensitive, not less—but there is a concomitant increase in
stability. This combination of seemingly opposed characteristics could well be accounted for if one assumes that TM pro-
motes fine adjustment. A finely adjusted system is, by definition,
one that is capable of registering fine differences in its environment and compensating for them; it *must* be sensitive, otherwise
it will not be able to respond. My thesis, in a nutshell, is that
TM tends to produce people who are simultaneously sensitive
and well balanced.

Both of these qualities are needed for a fully developed
human being. We speak of people as thin-skinned or thick-
skinned. The thick-skinned we tend to envy a little but also to
despise; we feel that they escape the minor irritations of life
but also miss its finer aspects. The thin-skinned, on the other
hand, we tend to pity; they over-react to situations, and lack
robustness. In their extreme forms, the thick-skinned person
goes trampling over everyone's feelings, while the thin-skinned
sits quivering in a corner.

The idea that strength and sensitivity are mutually incompatible has played a part in generating the myth of the suffering artist; certainly it is a consolation, if you are unhappy, to

believe that you are aesthetically (and even morally, for the two qualities are linked in many people's minds) superior to those who are relatively immune to pinpricks. Nevertheless, it would surely be desirable to have the best of both worlds—if that could be achieved.

TM, as I say, does seem to foster this kind of development. The effect can show itself in quite trivial ways, which are as much physiological as psychological. For example, when one is startled by a sudden loud noise, such as a car horn sounding nearby in the street, a number of physiological reactions normally follow: the heart speeds up, blood pressure increases, pupils dilate, and so on. These changes are part of the flight and fight reaction, which is a relic of our primitive life in the jungle. It is a generalized response to danger, and it prepares the body for action.

One current medical theory has it that an important cause of certain diseases, such as high blood pressure and coronary heart disease, is the frequent unnecessary turning on of this response in urban life. (Even watching an exciting film can do it.) If it were possible to reduce unnecessary responses of this kind, that would presumably be an advantage. This is a theme to which I shall return in Chapter Nine, but for the moment it is enough to notice that many meditators do find that the response to sudden loud noises and similar stresses is much more short-lived than it was before they meditated. This is *not*, let me repeat, because they do not register the event adequately—indeed, they may well say that they feel it more keenly than before; but within a few moments they have forgotten it, the body has reverted to its normal state (if, indeed, it ever left it), and the episode has ceased to have any effect.

The same increase in sensitivity coupled with improved balance seems to occur on the more characteristically psychological level as well. Stressful encounters with other people do occur, of course, and are keenly felt at the time, but once they are over they do not continue to obsess the mind so much as they would have done in the past.

Let me emphasize that these are gradual and long-term effects, and the rate at which they develop is very variable. I think, however, that they are the rule among people who have been practising TM for some time.

This is, of course, a subjective impression only, and so has little value scientifically. There is, however, as I shall show in Chapter Nine, a little evidence available from pilot studies which seems to support it. Moreover, it corresponds closely to the psychological changes which Maharishi has described as occurring on the way to enlightenment.

In the ordinary state—the state of ignorance—experiences are said to be like a line engraved on rock: deep and lasting, almost impossible to erase. As one continues to meditate, they become lighter and lighter. At first they change to a line on sand, and finally, in the fifth state (permanent Self-awareness) they are like a line on water, erased almost as soon as formed.

This is a psychological description, of course. But if enlightenment has a physiological basis, as Maharishi postulates, the story of Man Bahadur might well provide an important clue to understanding how the brain might evolve to give the psychological experience which Maharishi describes. Enlightenment, on this hypothesis, would be a state of perfect adjustment.

The more I thought about this idea, the more it seemed to make sense. Moreover, I began to see that the principle of fine adjustment did not apply only to the individual nervous system; it could also be fruitfully applied to the individual's interaction with the world. It seemed, in fact, to be a unifying concept of great power; it was like a skeleton key, which fitted a great number of locks. This encouraged me to believe that I was right in applying it to TM and SCI, for it is a central thesis of Maharishi's teaching that SCI is at the basis of all branches of knowledge. I therefore came to feel that I could use the principle of fine adjustment, not only to think about how the brain works in relation to TM, but also to understand the broader question of Maharishi's view of evolution. The whole of this book is really concerned with the principle of fine adjustment and its application.

In the next chapter I shall look at the principle of fine adjustment in general terms, as an introduction to the main part of my argument.

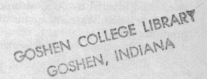

Holons, Hierarchies, and the Cycle of Differentiation

THE STORY OF Man Bahadur has given us the concept of fine adjustment. I now want to look at the process by which fine adjustment comes about.

Fine adjustment is achieved, I believe, through the operation of a particular process which I shall call the *cycle of differentiation*.[1] To avoid talking in generalities, I shall take a concrete example of how this works.

The Cycle of Differentiation

My illustration concerns the way a small business evolves to become a larger one. I choose a business for discussion because in a number of important respects it resembles a living organism: it exchanges material with its surroundings, it has component parts (staff) which interact with one another, it is born, develops, and dies. Both businesses and organisms, in fact, are "open dynamic systems".

Let us suppose that the business has been successful and finds itself taking on more work. This will mean that all the staff members have to do more; some find themselves overworked, and the directors therefore decide to expand by increasing the staff. The arrival of the new recruits eases the burden on the existing staff and increases the general efficiency of the organization; for a time everyone is satisfied. But no ideal state lasts for ever, and just because the capacity of the organization has been increased by its recent expansion it begins to accept new commitments and to branch out into new areas. Once again, the staff find themselves under strain, and new members have to be recruited. If this cycle continues to be repeated, the organization will grow within a few years from being a small concern, with perhaps ten or twenty members, to a much larger one employing hundreds or even thousands of people.

An organization which has evolved in this way may be said

to have become *differentiated*. When it was still quite small, the various staff members had to function in several different capacities: the boss often answered the telephone when no one else was in the office, and the secretary doubled as receptionist and tea-maker. As expansion occurs, however, people become more specialized: the boss is protected from the outer world by his personal secretary, typing is the responsibility of full-time audio-typists, and so on. Ideally, this specialization—differentiation—increases the efficiency and capacity of the organization immensely. (In practice, of course, it may not, but that is another story.)

Now, the point I want to emphasize is that the business has evolved in a cyclical fashion. First, there is a phase in which a lack is felt; people find themselves under pressure, mistakes are made, and there is a general sense of unrest. The solution is differentiation; jobs are split up, new staff is taken on. Eventually a new balance is struck, and harmony is restored. However, this ideal state does not last indefinitely. Just *because* the business has increased its capacity—and this is the point to notice particularly—it branches out in new directions, further demands are made upon it, and it has to differentiate itself still further.

It is important that I make this idea clear, because it is crucial to everything that follows; so please forgive me for dwelling on it at what may seem like inordinate length.

The phases of the cycle are as follows.

1. *Imbalance.* The demands of the situation are too much for the system, which is therefore thrown into some degree of disorder.
2. *Reorganization.* The system differentiates itself—becomes more complex—to take account of the demands being made on it. The result is
3. *Balance.* This, however, is temporary, because the differentiation which has given rise to balance has also brought about
4. *New Capacity.* This is very important. Because capacity has increased, new demands are made on the system and so the cycle begins to revolve once more.

In summary, the cycle of differentiation is the mechanism by which fine adjustment, and hence evolution, comes about. (Fig. 4.) The concept can be applied in a great variety of situations. Let us take human societies. A primitive society, such as a tribe, contains relatively few individuals, whose inter-relationships are fairly simple to study. Such a society can be effectively ruled by one man, or by a group of elders. A more complex society, like a modern industrial state, has far more components (individuals and groups) than does a primitive tribe, and so presents much greater administrative difficulties—balance is harder to achieve. To compensate, if balance *is* achieved, the society can achieve more than can the tribe. It can build cathedrals, or hospitals, or universities, it can explore the

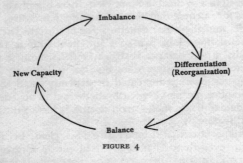

FIGURE 4

moon. (I am not concerned here with the question which form of society provides the greater measure of happiness for its members, or which is the better; I wish merely to point out the difference in complexity.)

If we now turn from the evolution of human societies to that of living organisms, we shall find that the cycle of differentiation is at work here also. The earliest organisms on earth, we assume, were single cells. Later, presumably, these developed into multicellular, jelly-like creatures, in which all the cells were more or less alike. But under the pressure of natural selection differentiation occurred, and cells became specialized into tissues and tissues ultimately into organs. All this early evolution must remain guesswork, for almost no trace of these primitive ancestors of ours has survived, and there is much dispute among experts about the details; but the general outline is almost certainly correct.

Evolution has occurred through an interplay between organisms and their environment; this much, at least, is certain. My point is that this interplay leads to a pattern of change which is *cyclical*. As an example, consider the emergence of life from the sea. The first colonists of the land, probably, were fishes which, like the present-day mud-skipper, could survive for long periods in pools which had dried up and could even hop about a little on their fins. They were driven ashore partly, perhaps, by a pioneering instinct, but partly also by the pressures of competition for food and danger from enemies. They were, in fact, in an imbalance phase of the cycle. Gradually there evolved species with stronger fins and the beginnings of lungs, and these could move about more freely in the new environment and survive longer away from the water. (There is, again, much dispute among experts about the genetic mechanisms which give rise to new species, but this need not detain us; I am concerned here only with the fact that new species did, somehow or other, arise.)

Each new evolutionary acquisition—primitive lungs, fins better adapted for walking, or whatever, can be described as reaching a new point of balance. The species which has achieved the new development can sit back thankfully for a moment in the race for survival; it is one up on everyone else, and for a while it can take things easy. But only for a while. Just *because* it can now do things which it could not do before, it finds itself facing new problems. A fish which has acquired limbs and primitive lungs has become an amphibian—it is in fact a newt. But newts, though they can live for long periods away from water, still have to keep their skins damp; newts cannot live in the desert. Many a primitive amphibian must have perished through over-adventurousness, by wandering too far from the water.

A few of those early frontiersmen, however, chanced to have skins which were less permeable to water than those of their relatives; hence they could conserve their precious supplies of body water a little longer. Over the unimaginable aeons of geological time, this characteristic became more and more accentuated through natural selection, and eventually the erstwhile amphibians found themselves transformed, not indeed into handsome princes, but at least into reptiles. Once again, a new point of balance had been reached.

My essential point is that *any* dynamic open system always evolves through this cyclical alternation between balance and imbalance, which brings about a constant trend towards complexity. It is the cycle of differentiation which has shaped us as we are today, and which is still shaping us. For the cycle of differentiation, as I hope to show in the course of this book, is the clue to the way in which we evolve, not only physically, but also psychologically and culturally.

Hierarchies[2]

Any system which evolves through the operation of the cycle of differentiation presents one most important and characteristic feature, namely, all such systems are arranged hierarchically, and the greater the degree of evolution the more elaborate the hierarchy.

The word hierarchy may be misleading. I do not mean to imply anything rigid or antiquated; quite the contrary, it is to their hierarchical arrangement that living systems owe their adaptability and flexibility. By hierarchy, I mean levels of complexity.

The metazoa—the multicellular organisms, such as ourselves —are all arranged hierarchically to a greater or lesser extent. In our own case, we are, of course, composed of cells, but the cells are very far from being all alike. They are differentiated into skin cells, nerve cells, kidney cells, muscle cells, and so on, and these are grouped together into tissues. The different kinds of tissues make up organs; thus the kidney, for example, is made up not only of various kinds of kidney cells but also of blood vessels, nerves, connective tissue, and so on, while the stomach contains smooth muscle, special lining membranes, nerves, blood vessels, and various other kinds of tissues. At the next level in the hierarchy, the various organs are grouped together into systems: the stomach, for example, forms part of the digestive system, together with the mouth, pharynx, oesophagus, intestines and so on. Finally, all the various systems, taken together, make up the whole organism.

At lower levels of evolution, differentiation is much less complete. Hydra, a little freshwater polyp which lives in ponds, has a net-like nervous system and muscle fibres, but there are no circulatory, respiratory, or digestive systems. This lack of specialization certainly limits Hydra's activities—it does little except move about, feed, and reproduce itself by the not very exciting method of budding—but one advantage is that Hydra has almost unlimited powers of regeneration—hence, of course, its name. To regrow a severed tentacle is nothing to Hydra; if you chop an animal into pieces, each will grow into a new individual, and even if you pass the creature through a sieve, so that all the cells become separated, they will join together into little clumps which quickly develop into reconstituted individuals.

In our case the story is very different. Our skin can repair itself pretty well, and even the liver can regrow and restore its architecture after damage, but the kidneys cannot (except to a very limited extent) and the same is true of muscle (including heart muscle) and brain. Lack of the ability to regenerate ourselves is the price we pay for the differentiation which has made us human.

Differentiation, then, results in the development of a hierarchical structure. To picture a hierarchy, imagine a tree, or a river with its tributaries, or the branching and sub-branching arrangement of the human arterial and venous systems. Such models can represent the "parts within parts" organization of atoms, or galaxies, or businesses, or organisms, or armies—the list could be extended indefinitely. It can also be applied to still more abstract concepts, such as the way in which we generate language. Indeed, once one begins to think in this way, one realizes that one is seeing a basic structural principle which underlies all orderly systems.

The unit in a hierarchy is what Arthur Koestler has called a holon—a useful term, which I shall adopt. A holon (from the Greek *holos*, meaning whole, with the suffix -on, as in proton) faces two ways, upwards and downwards. Looked at one way, it is an individual; looked at another, it is a component. A herring, for example, is a holon. In one way it is an individual, for it can be caught, cooked, and placed on your plate to be eaten. But it is also part of a group—the shoal—and, to the fisherman who catches it, it is not an individual but simply part of a mass in his net.

Our bodies, likewise, are made up of holons. Each cell is a holon; it is an individual, and yet it forms part of the tissue to which it belongs. Organs, too, are holons, and so are the various body systems. And each of us is a holon in our society; we are individuals, but also "members one of another".

Of all the systems which go to make up the body, the one which lends itself most easily and naturally to analysis in hierarchical terms is probably the nervous system. In primitive animals, as I have already remarked about Hydra, the nervous system is merely a network of cells scattered throughout the body. There is no headquarters of government. During the course of evolution, the nervous system has become more and more specialized, complex, and organized—in a word, differentiated—until it has reached the form it takes in ourselves. This has happened through the cycle of differentiation; it is the operation of the cycle which has produced our brains.

But the brain is not fixed for ever at birth; if it were, we could never learn anything. Whenever we learn, or reach a new insight, the brain, we assume, changes in some subtle way. And because we go on learning and solving problems all our lives, the brain, it seems, must remain capable of change for as long as we live.

This is a most exciting idea. It suggests that the focus of evolution—of Creative Intelligence—is the brain. Our evolution is more or less complete at birth except at the level of the brain; here, for us—and perhaps for the whole of life on this planet—is the growing point of evolution.

Let me clarify what I mean here by evolution. The word is commonly used in two different senses. To the biologist, evolution is concerned with genetics; species evolve but individuals do not. Thus it makes biological sense to talk of the evolution of *Homo sapiens* but not of the evolution of Tom Jones. The astronomer, on the other hand, talks of the evolution of the solar system or the universe; that is, of the evolution of a single entity. (The distinction I am making is between phylogeny and ontogeny.) SCI uses the term in both senses, because it regards the evolution of species and the development of individuals as aspects of the same basic life process—Creative Intelligence. (Many Western thinkers, of course, have adopted the same approach.)

In this book I, too, shall be using evolution to mean both kinds of development. This implies that the changes which occur in our brains when we learn and understand are evolutionary; evolution today is occurring principally in our brains.

This may seem a slightly unusual way of thinking about evolution, but I believe it is legitimate. Further justification for the idea comes from the common usage "cultural evolution". We are often told by biologists today that cultural evolution has replaced genetic evolution as the major force of change in the world; I think this is true, but cultural change, after all, arises from human thinking and produces changes in human awareness, and both thinking and awareness are presumably inscribed in the brain. Thus it is always to the brain that we must return; all of life's terror, mystery, and hope depends on that curious pinkish jelly we house in our skulls, and it is to our brains that we must look to understand what evolutionary change means today.

Summary

Fine adjustment comes about through the operation of the cycle of fine adjustment. This cycle underlies the whole evolutionary process. Its effect is to generate hierarchical systems composed of holons.

Roughly speaking, the complexity of an organism—the number of holons which go to make it up—is a measure of the extent to which it is evolved. There is a parallel here with human artefacts: good motor cars or radio sets, for example, tend to have more components, and to be more complex, than others; there is a sense in which high-quality products are more evolved. Similarly, with animals, the mammals are more complex than the reptiles, the reptiles are more complex than the amphibia, and so on. Within the group of mammals the differences are not well marked between species *except in the case of their brains*. This is particularly true of the higher mammals, such as the man-like apes. Admittedly there are certain important differences between ourselves and the apes as regards our feet and to a lesser extent our hands (we can oppose our thumbs, while apes cannot), but the similarities are much greater than the differences. The one way in which we really outshine our simian cousins is in having larger brains. And it is not purely a question of cerebral bulk; our brains are almost certainly more complex—they contain more components, much as a large radio contains more circuits and transistors than a smaller one.

If we use the word "evolution" in its wide sense, to cover ontogeny as well as phylogeny, evolution does not come to a stop at the moment we are conceived; it goes on, at least at the cerebral level, as long as we live. You cannot remember, learn, or think without modifying the structure of your brain at a subtle level, and this modification is evolution. It is against this background that I want to place TM.

TM is, I believe, a mechanism for enhancing the rate of evolution by speeding up the revolution of the cycle of differentiation.

PART TWO

V

The Brain: Core and Superstructure

THE EVOLUTION OF the human brain is arguably the most extraordinary biological event—apart from the origin of life itself—to have occurred on this planet. Not the least surprising feature of this evolution is the rapidity with which it took place —over a few million years, which is a mere clock-tick in geological time. In this chapter, I want to sketch the history of this remarkable organ, but first I shall say a few words about the main features it presents today.[1]

If you look at a human brain from above, you will see that it somewhat resembles a large walnut, in that its surface is sculpted into folds; like a walnut, too, it has a longitudinal cleft, which divides it incompletely into right and left cerebral hemispheres. The surface of the hemispheres is conventionally classified into various lobes, although the boundaries of these are somewhat artificial. An important landmark in this context is the central fissure, which separates the frontal lobe from the parietal lobe (fig. 5). As a rough approximation, one can say that the parts of the hemisphere in front of the central fissure are motor (concerned with movement), while those behind it are sensory (concerned with vision, hearing, and general sensation).

If you cut the brain open you would find that it is made up of two kinds of substance: grey matter and white matter. The microscope would show that the grey matter is chiefly composed of nerve cells and the white matter of nerve fibres. The fibres arise from the cells and travel to other parts of the brain or down the spinal cord, to end on other nerve cells which in turn give off fibres that pass out of the central nervous system to end in muscles, glands, or sense organs.

The anatomical nerves one sees with the naked eye are actually made up of large numbers of nerve fibres. The fibres are of two kinds; some take messages *from* the central nervous system to the effector organs (muscles and glands), while

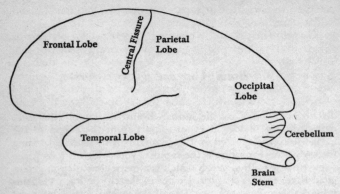

FIGURE 5   Side view of brain

others bring information *to* the central nervous system. Structurally, the two kinds of nerve fibre are just the same; the difference lies in the way in which they are connected within the brain. To this extent they resemble telephone wires, which are all made the same way but have different effects because they are connected differently. Each nerve cell makes connections with a great many others, and hence the nervous system is almost inconceivably complex.

The grey matter of the brain lies chiefly in a thin layer on the outside, where it is called the cortex (literally, bark). However, there are also important collections of nerve cells within the brain, and these are called nuclei.

The whole arrangement is something like that of an apple. The cortex is the skin, the nuclei are the pips, and the white matter is the pulp.

Like an apple, the brain has a stem. And just as the apple is, in a sense, an expansion of the top of the stem, so the brain is an expansion of the top of the spinal cord. If one follows the spinal cord upwards, it first becomes the brain stem and then disappears between the hemispheres, to become the "between-brain" (diencephalon). Here we find two very important structures: the thalamus—a bilateral group of nuclei lying at the centre of the brain—and just below it the hypothalamus. Projecting from the under-surface of the hypothalamus is another important structure, the pea-like pituitary gland, which hangs down on a short stalk (fig. 6).

The brain can be regarded as made up of two main elements. There is the core, which consists of the brain stem (medulla oblongata, pons, and midbrain), together with the thalamus and hypothalamus,* and there is the superstructure, consisting of the hemispheres, with their covering of cortex.

Now, this division corresponds closely to the way the brain has evolved. The core of the brain has undergone surprisingly few changes between the fishes and ourselves; the enormous

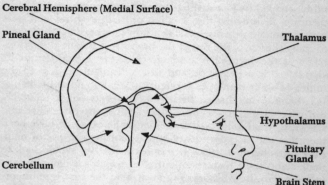

Cerebral Hemisphere (Medial Surface)

Pineal Gland

Thalamus

Hypothalamus

Pituitary Gland

Cerebellum

Brain Stem

FIGURE 6   Diagram to show position of those brain structures referred to in text

differences between our brain and the fish brain largely concern the development of the hemispheres—the superstructure. In fishes there is no true cerebral cortex. Primitive hemispheres first appear in amphibia and reptiles, but are apparently concerned only with the sense of smell. A true cortex is present

* From the functional point of view, one should also include in the core the limbic system. This is chiefly made up of "old" cortex—that is, it is the first cortex which was developed during evolution. In the human brain it becomes so distorted and compressed during growth that its anatomy is very hard to describe or visualize. Much of the limbic system lies in a semicircle in the cleft between the two cerebral hemispheres. There are many functional connections between the limbic system and the hypothalamus, which is why I am including it with the brain core.

in birds (which represent something of an evolutionary side-line) but only in the mammals does it begin to reach its full glory.

Much of this evolutionary sequence is recapitulated by the growing human embryo, for although the old idea that the embryo goes through all the steps of evolution is no longer tenable, there are some interesting correspondences. The cerebral hemispheres develop as outgrowths, or pouches, on either side of the tube that is destined to become the spinal cord and brain. At first they are small buds, but soon they become bigger and bigger, very much like the ears of those rabbit-shaped balloons which expand enormously as you blow them up. Before long they run out of room to grow, and start to curl round on themselves like a ram's horns, until they come to conceal most of the rest of the brain. It is the great development of the hemispheres which gives the human brain its characteristic appearance, and which distinguishes it from the brains of other mammals (except the whales and dolphins).

I want to emphasize the distinction between a relatively unchanged "old" core and a "new" superstructure, since it is crucial to what follows. It is the hemispheres which have been the great site of evolutionary activity during the rise of man, so presumably it is to the hemispheres that we should look to understand those features of ourselves which are characteristically human. But this does not mean that the core is unimportant—far from it. My main task in Part Two will be to examine the relationship between the old brain and the new.

Old Brain and New

It is at this point that we begin to encounter really profound difficulties, which are as much philosophical as scientific. For, to a surprisingly large extent, the functions you attribute to the various parts of the brain depend on how you think about human nature. A good example of this is provided by the theory advanced by a distinguished contemporary neuro-scientist, Paul MacLean, and enthusiastically championed by Arthur Koestler.[2]

MacLean thinks of the brain as made up of three units. The oldest part is what I have called the core, though without the limbic system; the core forms the "reptilian brain". Above it lies the "old mammalian" brain, consisting of the limbic system. At the third, and highest, level is the new brain, consisting of the hemispheres with their "new cortex".

As we have seen, there is no doubt that the brain has evolved in this general way. There is, however, a good deal of doubt about the conclusions which MacLean draws. He suggests that the two older parts of the brain—the reptilian and old mammalian brains—are between them responsible for all the less desirable aspects of human behaviour. Thus, the reptilian brain is hidebound and reactionary, a slave to precedent and instinct, while the old mammalian brain is the source of the emotions, which keep upsetting the behavioural applecart.

The new cortex is supposed to be the seat of the intellect, where rational decisions are taken. Unfortunately, communications between new cortex and the rest of the brain—especially the old cortex—are poor, and the result is a split in the mind based on a split in the brain—schizophysiology. Irrational impulses arise in the old brain, and these the new cortex tries to reason away—to rationalize. The impression one gets from reading MacLean's (and Koestler's) writings is of the new cortex as the type of the "cold scientist", hopelessly trying to perform intricate mathematical calculations from which he is incessantly distracted by the demands of a wayward, and rather backward, child.

Koestler has suggested that the only hope for humanity is to invent a pill to bridge the gap between the old brain and the new, and so to eliminate man's "paranoid streak". This idea seems to me to be precluded by the shortcomings of pharmacology; but even if it were not, the MacLean theory is, I believe, mistaken. It is really not much more than an old idea—that reason and emotion are totally opposed—dressed up in the robes of modern neurophysiology. I think that we ought to question the whole idea of this opposition.

There is actually quite a lot of evidence that human beings are *more* emotional than other mammals rather than less. Quite probably, the reason we seem to be comparatively little subject to emotion is that we have so designed our society that our emotional susceptibilities shall not be touched. (As just one example, notice how successfully we avoid thinking about death almost all the time in Western societies.)

Nigel Calder, to whom I am indebted for drawing my attention to the importance of emotion in human as compared with animal life, has rightly pointed out[3] that Western philosophy tends to look on reason as good and emotion as bad, yet far more damage has probably been done by reason than by emotion. Indeed, if civilization is finally wiped out by nuclear war, the fatal decision may be taken, not by a fallible human being at all, but by that emotion-free paragon, a computer.

I want to avoid the whole reason-emotion antithesis, and to suggest a different interpretation of the way the brain has evolved. I believe that all aspects of mental life, including both reason and emotion, are more highly developed in man than in other animals, and I think that the lesson we should draw from evolution is not that the development of the human brain has taken a wrong turning, as the Koestler-MacLean theory implies, but rather that development is not yet complete. What we need to do is to hurry it along.

Let us think once more about the way the brain has reached its present form. In evolutionary terms, it has been built up rather like one of those engineering construction kits you may have played with as a child. If you had such a kit, you will remember that the foundation is a basic set of parts which enables you to learn the principles of construction and to assemble a limited range of models. However, the instruction book also listed some more ambitious models, which unfortunately could be built only if you had some additional parts which came in a supplementary set. There were in fact a series of supplementary sets you could buy, each of which extended the range and complexity of the models you could construct.

This analogy is quite helpful in thinking about how the nervous system has evolved. Simple vertebrates, such as fish, have only the basic set—the core. More advanced creatures, such as reptiles, have the first supplementary set, which includes an elementary cortex. Mammals have a further supplementary set, which gives them a much better cortex and hence many more possibilities of behaviour. Man has the most advanced set of all, which includes a lot more cortex and greatly enlarges the scope of his behaviour.

As the mammalian cortex has evolved, it has acquired two characteristics which seem to be specially important. The first is the convolutions which are so prominent in the human brain and give it its typical crinkled appearance. The possession of convolutions appears to be related to intelligence; the rat, for example, has no convolutions, but the cat and dog have some and the ape has many more, while whales and dolphins rival ourselves in this respect. The convolutions greatly increase the effective area of the cortex.

The second feature of the evolving brain to which I want to draw attention is the development of what might be called "uncommitted" cortex—that is, cortex which is not obviously concerned with sensation or movement. Possession of such areas seems to be closely bound up with the capacity for abstract thought. The frontal zones seem to be specially important in this respect. These are the areas lying right at the front of the brain, beyond those sites where stimulation gives rise to movement (see fig. 5). The frontal zones are much larger in ourselves than in the higher apes, and even in ourselves they do not become fully ready for use until the age of four to seven years.[4] For a long time they were called silent, because no function could be assigned to them. Now, however, it is believed that they are necessary for the formation of long-term plans and strategies, and of course the ability to anticipate the future in this way is one of the attributes which distinguish us most clearly from other mammals. The frontal zones are thus of very great importance.

From what I have said so far, it is evident that the cortex is an extraordinary evolutionary acquisition. But what is its real function? From many books one gets the impression that the cortex is the site of thought and intellect, and these are usually equated unhesitatingly with consciousness. But let us look at this idea a little more closely.

Consciousness is at once the most fundamental feature of our experience, the one essential "given" from which everything else stems, and the most elusive of all concepts to describe or pin down. Only time, perhaps, begins to approach consciousness in mysteriousness. Certainly we are unimaginably far from being able to say what is the relation between brain activity and consciousness. And yet, one or two facts do emerge.

The most important of these, I think, is that we can distinguish, in brain terms, between the *fact* of consciousness and its *content*. Consciousness as such does not seem to be produced by the cortex; at least, it is possible to damage the cortex severely without thereby destroying consciousness. Lesions of the core, however, do produce unconsciousness. It seems, in fact, that the maintenance of awareness depends, at least partially, on an interplay of impulses between a scattered network of cells in the core known as the reticular formation and higher parts of the core such as the thalamus.[5] (Consciousness therefore seems to depend on feedback loops.)

Unless, like Descartes, one insists on denying consciousness to lower animals, this arrangement is surely just what one might expect. If consciousness is really an emergent property of life, and begins far down the evolutionary scale, it would be reasonable to expect that its manifestation would be bound up with the oldest parts of the brain. And this is just what we do find.

What, then, is the function of the cerebral hemispheres—the proud new brain? The answer seems to be that they are chiefly responsible for the *content* of consciousness. Having an elaborate cortex increases the extent to which consciousness can reflect the outer world and respond to it. The cortex, in other words, is responsible for the finer details of perception, thought, and action.

It is perfectly true that all the most important features of our experience depend on the cortex. But this should not blind us to the fact that all the magnificent achievements of the cortex are founded on the activity of the older parts of the brain. The cortex, in a nutshell, acts as a fine tuning device on the rest of the brain, increasing its sensitivity and adaptability.

If one compares the mind to an organ, the core would be the organ pipes and the bellows which supply them with compressed air, while the hemispheres would be the keys, stops, and pedals needed to modulate the flow of air to produce the music. Without the core, the proud new brain would be as useless as an organ without compressed air.

In so far as our being has a centre at all, it is the brain core. Wilder Penfield, the scientist and neurosurgeon whose classic studies of the exposed human brain at operation have shed a quite special light on this fascinating subject, has written as follows:

It is clear that the most important means of co-ordinating the function of cortical areas is not the association mechanisms within the cortex. Such co-ordination is provided largely by the integrating action of subcortical centres which must lie within the mesencephalon [midbrain] and the diencephalon.

Therefore, if the term "seat of consciousness" is to be used at all, it must be applied to the old brain, for the diencephalon is "that nervous centre to which ... the most heterogeneous impressions are brought". From it must go out effector neuronal impulses that are capable of summoning a memory, of causing the lips to speak, or the arm to move.[6]

It is difficult to avoid the impression that many writers on the brain—especially the authors of popular books on the subject—are so obsessed with man as a thinker that they overestimate the importance of the cortex. It is, of course, perfectly true that the mental activities which make us human depend on the cortex, but it does not follow that the cortex in some way rules the brain. I am sure that Penfield is right to emphasize the importance of the old brain; in so far as the brain has a ruler at all, it is the core. We might perhaps picture the core as a monarch, who governs his kingdom with the assistance of advisers. As his country has grown and become more complex, so he has needed more advisers—hence the growth of the cortex. The monarch, however, remains the ruler.

I do not want to over-emphasize this idea, or to give the impression that I am trying to locate consciousness in the brain core. The brain acts as a whole, and all its parts are interdependent. In many ways a good analogy for the brain is an ecology, in which the various species (parts) interact to give an over-all balance. But the rôle of the core is crucial.

The Difference Between the two Hemispheres

Before concluding this anatomical chapter, I want to say something about the functional difference between the left and right hemispheres, for this is an important development at the human level.

In right-handed people, the left hemisphere controls speech and therefore is said to be dominant. (In general, each hemisphere controls the opposite side of the body.) The functions of the right hemisphere are rather difficult to study, but appear to be concerned with the representation of space; for example, the ability to carry a mental map of your house and its surroundings seems to depend on the right hemisphere.

Classically, the left hemisphere, being the one which has access to speech, has been considered the site of the higher intellectual functions, the right hemisphere being looked on as a poor relation. More recently, some people have suggested that we over-value the left hemisphere in the West because of our obsession with logical (verbal) thought, and this has led to the notion that other cultures, especially the Eastern ones, lay more emphasis on right hemisphere function. The role of meditation is thus conceived to be the restoration of the right hemisphere to its proper status, and the ideal human condition is supposed to be one in which both hemispheres co-operate fully and equally.[7]

This is in some ways an attractive notion, with its implication that the cultural meeting between East and West is reflected in the anatomical meeting between the two hemispheres of our brains. I cannot help feeling myself that it is oversimple, but then we know that the greatest insights often look very simple once they have been attained. It does seem, in fact, that there are at least two distinct modes of thinking open to the human mind. One, hitherto dominant in the West, is that of Aristotelian logic, with its emphasis on either-or and the excluded middle. This form of thinking leads eventually to a picture of the universe as composed of atoms, immutable and indivisible.

The other form of thinking has been called co-ordinative or associative. It is concerned, not with things, but with patterns, and it leads to a picture of the universe as built up of waves. Modern science seems to be moving increasingly towards the second kind of world picture.[8]

In practice, we need both kinds of thinking, and I am sure that those who emphasize the desirability of counter-balancing the typical Western preference for either-or logic with co-ordinative thinking are right. Whether this is simply a question of which hemisphere to use, however, seems to me more doubtful. In any case, if that idea does turn out to be right, it will complement my hypothesis rather than conflict with it. So far as TM is concerned, there is, as I shall point out in Chapter Nine, a little evidence that synchronization between left and right sides of the brain does occur, and this would agree with the two-hemispheres idea. But I do not think that our understanding of the brain is yet sufficient for us to say more.

Summary

Two main points emerge from what I have said in this chapter.

First, the function of the cortex is to act as a fine tuning mechanism on the brain core, and so to increase the range of activities of which the core is capable.

Second, the cortex has evolved in a remarkable fashion over a comparatively short time. This implies that the cycle of differentiation has been at work on the brain; and if, as I have suggested, the evolution of our brains is not yet complete, the cycle must be at work still.

In the next two chapters, I want to examine these ideas in greater detail.

VI

Cybernetics

THE CONCEPTS OF fine tuning and of the cycle of differentiation both derive from the typically twentieth-century science of cybernetics. In this chapter, I want to look at cybernetics and at what it implies for our understanding of the brain.

First, what is cybernetics?

The word *cybernétique* was coined in 1834 by the French mathematician and physicist A. M. Ampère (whose own name is commemorated in our "amp"), and was used by him to mean "science of government". At the time the word did not catch on, but "cybernetics" was reintroduced independently by the American mathematician Norbert Wiener in his book of that name, first published in 1948. Wiener derived the word from the Greek *chubernetes*, meaning a steersman, and defined the subject in a subtitle as "control and communication in the animal and the machine".

Cybernetics, in fact, is concerned with ideas such as feedback and self-government, and therefore has the widest possible ramifications not only in engineering (where the concepts were first formulated) but also in biology, psychology, and even politics and economics. Wiener himself did not hesitate to apply them to very basic questions about the nature of life and mind, and others have been equally enthusiastic. "Cybernetics," Gregory Bateson has said, "is the biggest bite out of the fruit of the Tree of Knowledge that mankind has taken in the last two thousand years."[1] That statement may sound a little overdramatic, yet I think it may well prove not to have been an exaggeration. For cybernetics is the first application in science of what I have called correlative thinking; that is, it deals with relationships, order, and pattern—ideas which have hitherto been relatively neglected in the West.

Cybernetics and its applications have become highly technical subjects in the hands of specialists, but for present purposes, fortunately, it is the principles we require, not the details; and the principles could hardly be simpler.

Self-Regulation and Feedback

Elementary cybernetic mechanisms have been with us for a long time. A familiar example is the ball-cock on a cold water cistern. This consists of a float mounted on an arm which operates a valve. When water is removed from the cistern, the float falls and opens the valve, so that the cistern begins to fill up again. When the float reaches its original level the valve closes and the water supply is shut off.

Another example of the same principle is the governor of a steam engine. This is a valve which opens or closes automatically, according to the speed of the engine, being operated by weights mounted on rods attached to a rotating shaft. The faster the shaft rotates, the further the weights move outwards under centrifugal force, and this movement closes the valve and shuts off the supply of steam. A governor of this kind tends to keep engine speed constant, regardless of load.

The feature which all such systems have in common is that information is *fed back* to whatever is producing the action, so that *action is influenced by its own results*. What information means in this context is perhaps best expressed in Bateson's phrase "news of a difference". The ball-cock allows water to flow when the level in the cistern is different from the correct level, and the governor acts to restore engine speed to its correct value whenever a difference from that value occurs.

In both the examples I have given, the systems tend to oppose any change that occurs. Water level and engine speed remain more or less constant. Feedback systems of this kind are called negative. So far as the body is concerned, negative feedback is specially important, because it is negative feedback which is needed for self-regulation.

Positive feedback would, of course, be the opposite. It would occur in a system in which any change tended to augment itself. Mechanical examples are not so easy to find, but an unfortunately familiar economic example is provided by inflation: the more prices rise, the more people demand higher wages to keep pace, and so the faster prices rise. (Economics, as I have mentioned, provides a good example of the application of cybernetic principles.) In general, any vicious circle (or virtuous circle too, for that matter) is an instance of positive feedback. In Chapter Two I suggested that TM works by positive feedback, in that the increasing attractiveness of the subtler layers of experience draws the attention on faster the nearer it approaches the level of pure awareness. (But notice that there is also an element of negative feedback in TM, since any incipient deviation from the trend towards subtler layers of experience is automatically countered by the attraction of those layers.)

Although sometimes desirable, positive feedback is often a source of instability. It occurs, for example, in an overloaded amplification system, where it produces an unpleasant howl. It also occurs in a car with loose steering: each correction that the driver applies comes too late, so that he has to make a larger correction in the opposite direction; thus the wobble builds up progressively until there is a disaster. The spread of rumours is yet another example of the same effect; each person who passes the story on distorts it a little more, until eventually it becomes wildly exaggerated and entirely different from what it was at first. Unstable systems of this kind are said to have gone into "runaway".

Self-Regulating Systems and the Brain—the Concept of Plan
The relevance of self-regulating systems operating on negative feedback for our understanding of living organisms will now, I hope, be apparent. What man-made automata and organisms have in common is that their activities are governed by *Plans*.

I have borrowed the concept of Plan from Miller, Galanter, and Pribram,[2] because it seems to me a very valuable and illuminating one. A Plan is a sequence of instructions for achieving a particular end. Plans may be simple, or they may be complex, in which case they are built up of hierarchies of sub-Plans.

The humble ball-cock in your cistern has one very simple Plan—to keep the water level constant. An anti-aircraft missile homing on a target has a Plan too: to pursue its quarry until it catches it, regardless of any manœuvres the quarry may make to shake it off. But the Plan of the missile is much more complex than that of the ball-cock, and so it contains a number of sub-Plans. If the aircraft turns, the missile must turn also; if the aircraft dives, the missile must dive, and so on.

The last few decades have seen an extraordinary proliferation in the development of self-guiding automata, and, as one might expect, much of this technology has been military. There are bombers which fly supersonically at a couple of hundred feet, guided by computers through valleys, round hills, and over power lines; there are clustered warheads inside missiles which have eyes and are programmed to look for tanks, on which they home selectively, ignoring lorries, houses, and rocks. The list could go on and on, but the essential point is that we now have machines with built-in goals which they pursue with great sophistication and refinement.

All this sophistication is based on computer science; that is, on cybernetics. All complex self-regulating machines contain computers, and the computers have sets of instructions—Plans —to cover the various eventualities which may occur.

The resemblances between such man-made automata and living creatures are obvious enough, and it is natural to suppose that the analogy is more than just an analogy. The brain, it would seem, is a computer, and contains Plans and sub-Plans to guide the organism through life.

I want to look at this idea in a little more detail, to see how far it holds good and what it implies. I shall start by considering an aspect of brain function, namely temperature regulation, which almost certainly does lend itself very easily to discussion as a self-regulating system.

Temperature Regulation as Plan

The over-all Plan for temperature regulation is quite simple: to keep body temperature roughly constant (in our own case, at about 37 degrees Centigrade). How is this achieved?

The answer is, by feedback. The temperature-regulating system of the body is quite closely analogous to that of a domestic heating and air-conditioning system which is designed to maintain an even temperature in the house, summer and winter. A house fitted with such a system contains a thermostat—that is, a temperature-controlled switch. When the temperature falls, the thermostat switches on the central heating; when the temperature reaches its correct value, the thermostat switches the heating off. If, in summer, the temperature rises above the desired value, the thermostat switches on the air conditioning until the temperature falls to the correct value once more.

We have here a feedback loop, in which the effects of heating or cooling the house, as the case may be, react on the system via the thermostat to maintain a balance.

Body temperature is regulated in much the same way. The hypothalamus contains cells which act as a thermostat and are sensitive to the temperature of the blood flowing through the region. If this temperature falls, the hypothalamus switches on various heating devices throughout the body; if the temperature rises, it switches the heating mechanisms off, and if the rise is marked it brings cooling mechanisms into play as well.

The over-all Plan is thus to maintain body temperature constant; this purpose is served by various sub-Plans for heating and cooling. The cooling sub-Plans include sets of instructions for increasing the amount of blood flowing to the surface of the body and for sweating; in dogs, they include panting, but in human beings this is an emergency Plan only. The heating sub-Plans, on the other hand, include decreasing the amount of blood flowing to the surface, shivering, and increasing the output of thyroid hormone (which raises the metabolic rate and so causes more heat production).*

What I have just described is by no means the whole story of temperature regulation; there are many more sub-Plans, which have the effect of making the system as a whole more finely adjusted, more capable of maintaining an even temperature in all circumstances.

* The thyroid hormone mechanism is specially interesting because it provides an excellent and well-understood example of how feedback operates in the body. The output of thyroid hormone (and indeed of most other hormones) is regulated by a feedback cycle involving the pituitary gland, which, you may remember, is situated just below the hypothalamus. The pituitary produces a "thyroid stimulating hormone" which causes the thyroid to release thyroid hormone; and the rate at which the pituitary releases this stimulating hormone is governed by the amount of thyroid hormone in the blood. Hence the loop is closed and the production of thyroid hormone (and so the metabolic rate) is held constant, unless —as happens in prolonged exposure to cold—the regulating system is over-ridden by the hypothalamus.

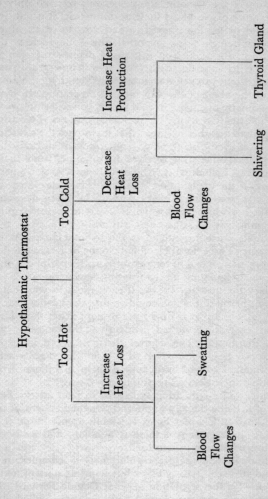

FIGURE 7 The Hierarchy of Temperature Control

For example, the hypothalamus does not respond only to the temperature of the blood flowing through it; if it did, the system would be far too insensitive and slow to react. Many other factors influence the hypothalamus—one such is the temperature of the skin. You can easily demonstrate this in yourself by lying in a hot bath until your temperature rises. If you now get out, you will start to sweat as your hypothalamus responds to the abnormally high blood temperature. If, however, you immerse one hand in cold water, you will stop sweating. The information from your cold hand alters the setting of the hypothalamic thermostat so that it switches the sweating mechanism off even though body temperature is still raised.

The hypothalamus also receives information from many other sources, including psychological information—here, presumably, is the explanation for the Tibetan art of *tumo*. It seems, in fact, that almost every part of the brain has some effect on the hypothalamus—which is why temperature regulation in mammals is so exquisitely accurate.

Thermostats are not confined to the hypothalamus. As we saw in Chapter Three, local blood flow to the fingers and toes is important in the control of temperature at the periphery, and there are local regulating mechanisms in these areas which act as subsidiary thermostats. It is as if each room in your house had its own thermostat which could control the flow of heat to that room alone. But it is important to notice that these local thermostats do not operate independently of the central, hypothalamic, thermostat. The central thermostat can influence their response level; moreover, the local thermostats send back information to the brain and so help to influence the hypothalamic thermostat. The traffic is two-way.[3]

The temperature-regulating system is, in fact, an excellent example of a hierarchically organized dynamic system of the kind I outlined in Chapter Four. It is built up of a number of interlocking cycles; each of these is a holon, and so is the temperature-regulating system itself.

For, although temperature regulation is so complex, it is not an end in itself. It is a Plan, but it forms part of a still larger Plan—for the regulation of what Claude Bernard, the great nineteenth-century French physiologist, called the "internal environment".

The Internal Environment

Life began in the sea, and for a primitive creature the water provided a near-perfect environment. Its temperature is almost constant; it brings oxygen and nutrients; it removes waste matter. All the needs of the cell, in fact, are catered for by the sea.

As animals grew larger, however, the water could not reach every cell so easily; moreover, as cells became more specialized they became more demanding about their environment. Hence there arose the need for a special circulation to bathe each cell in an ideal fluid matrix. This was the internal environment. To preserve its constancy, animals developed impermeable skins and acquired special regulatory mechanisms such as kidneys and gills. And when our ancestors left the sea and took to the land, they carried with them, enclosed within their skins, the internal environments which had been formed in the course of evolution. It used to be said that the composition of our own body fluids today is the same as that of the primeval sea from which we came. Unfortunately this romantic idea can no longer be fully sustained, but it remains true that the constancy of the internal environment is the first necessity of life. Even small deviations from ideal values for temperature, acidity-alkalinity (pH), and the concentration of dissolved elements such as sodium and potassium produce disease or death, and the body has therefore developed immensely sophisticated methods of regulating these values accurately.

When an animal finds itself in a situation where the stability of its internal environment is threatened, it can do one of two things. It can make the best of the position, by putting up with the changes and allowing its temperature, say, to fluctuate with that of the environment (that is, it may conform), or it can try to control its internal environment actively, to keep it constant in the face of outer changes (regulation). In general, the more evolved an animal is, the more likely is it to be a regulator. Regulation seems to confer evolutionary advantage. Thus, the reptiles were one up on the amphibia because, among other advantages, they had impermeable skins which conserved their precious body water and so allowed them to move inland. Similarly, the mammals and birds had the edge on the reptiles because they could regulate their internal temperature and so survive in situations which were too extreme for the conforming reptiles.

The way in which the body regulates the internal environment has been given the name homeostasis; derived from the Greek, this means "staying the same". The word "homeostat" has also been coined (by analogy with thermostat) to mean any physiological mechanism which regulates homeostasis. In higher animals, the headquarters of the regulating system is the hypothalamus, which contains a great many homeostats controlling not only temperature but also body water content, blood glucose concentration, and a number of other features of the internal environment. The individual activities of all these homeostats are orchestrated by the brain to produce the symphony of homeostasis as a whole.

The question now arises, have we at this point reached a summit in the hierarchy of organization? By no means. The regulation of the internal environment is an enormously complicated affair, but even so it is not an end in itself. It forms a sub-Plan of a still larger Plan, which comprises the activities of the organism as a whole. In Man Bahadur's case, for example, the only reason he could survive in the cold of the Himalayas was because his temperature regulation was so finely adjusted, but that information does not tell us everything we want to know about him. He was not living up in the snows for the sake of his temperature-regulating apparatus; why was he there? The answer is that he had gone into the mountains for religious reasons; that is, he had a still larger Plan, of which his ability to withstand cold was only one component, although admittedly a necessary one.

This is true of all mammals and birds: they have laid down in their brains Plans based on feedback for regulating their internal environment, but they have done so only as a means to an end—the freeing of their energies to attend to other, more interesting, matters in the *external* environment, such as courtship, hunting, and—in our own case—science, philosophy, art, and religion.

And here we reach the real crux of the matter. Temperature control is a holon, a sub-Plan in the larger Plan for regulating the internal environment. Regulation of the internal environment, again, is a sub-Plan in larger Plans for activities in the external environment. Now, we have seen that cybernetics tells us a great deal about the mechanics of control of the internal environment; may it not do so for the external environment too? In other words, is our every-day behaviour a cybernetically-based affair?

Plans and the External Environment

Some thinkers, notably Miller, Galanter, and Pribram, have in fact suggested that the concept of Plan applies to the external environment as well as the inner one (indeed, most of the discussion in *Plans and the Structure of Behaviour* is concerned with the outer environment). To give an idea of what this implies, I shall take the process of pumping up a bicycle tyre and analyse it in terms of Plan.

When you take your bicycle out, after having left it in the shed for some time, you usually test its tyres for hardness with your thumb. If you find that a tyre is too soft, you give it a few strokes with the pump; then you test it again and, if necessary, pump a bit more, until the requisite degree of hardness is achieved.

Notice that an essential step in this sequence is periodic testing. If you do not test the tyre at intervals, but merely continue to pump, the result will be a burst tyre. In other words, feedback—knowledge of the results you are achieving—is a vital part of pumping, and if you were asked to give instructions to the proverbial man from Mars on how to pump up a tyre you would have to remember to include testing. (Fig. 8.)

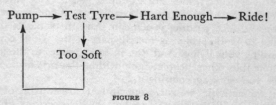

Pump —→ Test Tyre —→ Hard Enough —→ Ride!

Too Soft

FIGURE 8

And further refinements, such as what to do if the tyre turns out to have a puncture, could be included. The result would be a "flow chart" or hierarchy of sub-Plans to cover all the eventualities of pumping.

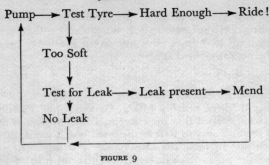

FIGURE 9

It may sound rather absurd to analyse a simple process like pumping up a tyre in this way, but, as Miller and his colleagues remark in connection with their own example (hammering), it is better to amuse the reader than to baffle him. And although the example is simple, the Plan concept can be extended upwards into the highest realms of human thought and activity.

Suppose that instead of breaking pumping down into its component sub-routines we see how it fits into larger patterns. We can do this because pumping is a holon. It is not an end in itself, but makes sense only as part of a larger whole—riding the bicycle. Riding could also be analysed into a number of sub-Plans, such as pedalling, keeping one's balance, steering, and so on, but let us leave that aspect aside and continue the hierarchy upwards.

Riding, like pumping, is not an end in itself, but has its place in a larger whole. For example, you may be riding the bicycle to get to work, or to keep fit (or, of course, for both reasons at once); riding is a holon. And the same is true of getting to work, which is merely part of the whole complex of earning your living. And *that*, in turn, relates to the jobs of innumerable other people, both within the organization for which you work and outside it.

All the activities we carry out, in fact, are capable of being described as Plans. Each of us has a vast repertoire of Plans stored within us, ready to be used if the appropriate circumstances should arise.

What we have here is essentially a cybernetic description of behaviour. The mechanisms which control the internal environment can be thought of as carrying out Plans, and their goal is the completion of a Plan—for example, the attainment of a stable body temperature. But the same is true of the mechanisms responsible for behaviour in the external world, except that here the goal, and hence the Plan, are different.

On the present hypothesis, all the Plans we use are recorded somehow or other in the brain. This implies that the brain is a cybernetically constructed mechanism, analogous to the computers which guide missiles and so on. But what evidence is there for this idea?

This is a very large question, about which the experts disagree. It is much too technical to discuss in detail here—the bibliography will give some suggestions for further reading—but, in very impressionistic terms, the picture which seems to be emerging is something like this.

1. *The Motor System.* There are within the muscles remarkable devices called spindles, which continuously measure the degree of stretch within the muscle and also the rate at which that stretch is changing. The spindles thus act as sensing devices, feeding back information about the muscles to the spinal cord and brain. The brain uses this information to compute the changes in muscular contraction which are needed to maintain posture and for walking and moving.

But there is more to the spindles than that. They are themselves miniature muscles, with their own motor nerve supply and capable of contracting independently of the main muscle in which they lie. If they contract, their tension increases, and information about this is signalled back to the brain via the sensory nerve. Hence the spindles can be "set" by the central nervous system, like adjustable triggers, according to the needs of the body as a whole. That is why you jump at the least sound when you are very tense; the muscular system is then set very finely, like a gun with a hair trigger.

Thus we see that the brain can actively control the kind of information which it receives from the muscles, and this in turn affects the control of the muscular system. Exactly how this arrangement accounts for our behaviour is still uncertain, but the suggestion is that what controls our actions from moment to moment is a Plan—what Pribram calls an "Image of Achievement" which is formed, also from moment to moment, in the classic motor areas of the brain, just in front of the central fissure. These Plans are continually being modified by incoming information from the muscle spindles and elsewhere, and their probable results are computed forward in time by the cerebellum (the little brain, which is attached to the back of the brain stem, just below the occipital lobe). Such forward computing goes on all the time, but we are happily unaware of it until it goes wrong. A common experience which illustrates this is treading on a non-existent top step when going upstairs in the dark. Another is what happens when one misjudges the weight of an object one wants to lift; if one over-estimates it, the object flies up into the air, while if one under-estimates it, the object appears for a moment to be immovably fixed to the table.

Longer-term Plans may be formed and stored in the forward parts of the frontal lobes, which, as I have said, are exceptionally well developed in human beings. The advantage of possessing these areas seems to be that they permit the building up of complex Plans. An important consequence of this idea is that all our behaviour, all our Plans, are in a sense elaborations of motor sequences. In other words, the hierarchical structure of behaviour which I have proposed seems to be reflected in the organization of the brain.

2. *The Sensory System.* The sensory pathways bring visual, auditory, and other information to the brain. Classically, this transmission was regarded as a passive affair; the real work began only when the information reached the cortex, where it was analysed, compared, and evaluated.

Today, a rather different view of perception seems to be developing. According to this view, perception is not passive but active; the brain *selects* what matters to it according to the bias which has been partially built into it at birth and partially acquired subsequently, through experience—and which is constantly altering under the influence of experience. The state of our brains, in other words, decides how they register the world (an important idea from the viewpoint of SCI).

In outline, the arrangement is as follows. There are numerous filters in the sensory pathways, and the sensitivity of these filters can be "set" by other brain areas. One such area is the reticular formation, which, as I mentioned in Chapter Five, is concerned with the maintenance of wakefulness. But the cortex, too, seems to play an important part in this setting, and indeed Pribram has suggested that this is the function of the so-called association areas of the cortex. These are the areas of uncommitted cortex which are so plentiful in the human brain. The classic view is that they are responsible, as the name implies, for the assembling of different kinds of information. But Pribram has suggested that their real function is to set the filters, and so actively to influence the amount and kind of information reaching the brain.[4]

If these ideas are right, we arrive at an interesting conclusion: the so-called motor and sensory systems are really quite similar to one another in the way they are built. Thus, the motor system has been described by Pribram as a "sensory system for action", while the sensory system is also motor. For example, many of the nerve fibres which come from the temporal cortex (a sensory area) are connected, not to the thalamus, as one would expect if they were sensory, but to motor nuclei in the centre of the brain; and electrical stimulation of the temporal cortex can affect the way in which impulses are transmitted along the visual pathways from retina to occipital cortex.[5] To put it crudely, the temporal cortex seems to be like a dial which can be used to adjust the sensitivity of the visual system. But this is a feedback arrangement, because the setting of the temporal lobe dial is itself *decided by* incoming (sensory) information. As one eminent researcher, Robert B. Livingstone, has put it: "The nervous system appears to be made up less of independent linear pathways than of mutually interdependent loop circuits which stitch together the various parts of the brain into a functional whole."[6]

Perhaps I could summarize the situation by saying that the over-all picture of the brain which I get from reading the writings of many modern authorities is of a cybernetically designed structure, which has evolved by the progressive addition of finer and finer control mechanisms, of which the new cortex is the most sophisticated and most recently acquired.

Now, some people may feel that all such mechanistic descriptions of behaviour and its brain substrate are misleading because they fail to do anything like justice to the richness of our behaviour, thoughts, and imagination. What can cybernetics tell us about how Shakespeare wrote his sonnets? I find it difficult not to sympathize with this attitude, and yet I feel it is, at least partially, based on a misunderstanding about the concept of mechanism. To show why, I shall put the computer-brain analogy in its historical context.

Understanding the Brain—the Choice of a Model

In general, when we try to understand how something works, we do so by building a model—if not in actual material, at least conceptually. Thus, we often compare the various organs of the body to human artefacts. The heart, for example, we call a pump, and indeed a pump it is. Similarly, the kidney is a filter, the liver a factory, and so on. All these analogies are partially metaphorical, and must not be pushed too far. Each of the organs I have mentioned (except perhaps the heart) has subsidiary functions which are not covered by the metaphor; thus the kidney secretes hormones, and even its filtration is not merely passive but is active and dynamic. Still, the metaphors we use are valuable and accurate for many purposes.

In the case of the brain the problem is much more difficult. For Aristotle, the brain was an organ for cooling the blood; and even when its function as the regulator of muscular activity became recognized, the question of choosing the right metaphor to picture its working remained. The earliest attempts to represent the functioning of the nervous system in mechanical terms were made in the seventeenth century, when the nerves were thought to be hollow and filled with fluid which was stored in the brain and forced down into the muscles to make them expand. This was a hydraulic model, which pictured the neuromuscular system as something like the braking system of a modern car. Descartes adopted a nervous system model of this kind.

Unfortunately, it was soon shown that the muscles lost volume when they shortened, whereas the hydraulic theory, of course, predicted that they should expand. The hydraulic theory therefore had to be abandoned; but no satisfactory alternative could be suggested in the light of the technology of the time.

The discovery of electricity and the subsequent invention of the telephone provided quite new possibilities. What could be more natural than to suppose that the brain was built like a telephone exchange, in which incoming information was suitably directed to the muscles via outgoing pathways? Support for this concept came from the finding that electrical changes did, in fact, occur in the nerves when they carried impulses. To be sure, there was the embarrassing question of the telephone operator, which seemed to require a "ghost in the machine", but before long automatic telephone exchanges were invented, and all seemed to be well.

However, it was evident to many people that the brain did a great deal more than merely re-route incoming impulses. It took information in and recombined it in various ways; it built up patterns, and generated complexity in a manner which no telephone exchange, however elaborate, could do. A new model was therefore needed.

Then came computers, and at last, so it seemed, we had the right model for the brain. Today, analogies from computer terminology are freely used in discussions about the brain, and various aspects of brain function are simulated on computers, the underlying assumption often being that if the same result is achieved by the brain and by the computer then brain and computer must work on much the same principles. The brain, in fact, is simply a super-complex computer.

Some cyberneticists, including Wiener himself, have held that the new science disposes once and for all with the ancient debate between mechanists and vitalists, because there is no essential difference between a living creature and a self-regulating automaton except—so far—one of complexity.

> The many automata of the present age are coupled to the outside world both for the reception of impressions and for the performance of actions. They contain sense organs, effectors, and the equivalent of a nervous system to integrate the transfer of information from one to the other. They lend themselves very well to description in physiological terms. It is scarcely a miracle that they can be subsumed under one theory with the mechanisms of physiology. . . . In fact, the whole mechanist-vitalist controversy has been relegated to the limbo of badly posed questions.[7]

One of the principal arguments of the vitalists was that living creatures differed from non-living systems in having purposes. An animal seeks to hide from its enemies, to eat, and to reproduce itself, and we call these activities purposive. Until quite recently it seemed that human artefacts lacked purposes, but this is no longer entirely true. The purpose of a cistern ball-cock is to keep the water level constant. This is admittedly a very simple instance of purpose; but what about the guided missile pursuing an aircraft? How does it differ in principle from a dog chasing a rabbit? Is not the difference between living and non-living systems largely one of complexity? Various scientific toys have been built which do, in fact, carry out many of the activities of simple living creatures— exploration, food-finding, shelter-seeking and so on.

Ever since Descartes, rationalists have been trying to show that animals (and ultimately human beings) are automata. The mechanical devices of the seventeenth century were far too crude to make this idea seem plausible, and moreover they were designed to imitate the superficialities of human behaviour—walking, grasping, talking, and so on—rather than the fundamentals, such as purpose. Those of the twentieth are very different. Today the argument has subtly shifted its ground. The older rationalists were concerned to show that animals and human beings did not really have purposes but merely seemed to do so. The modern rationalist can cheerfully concede that living creatures do have purposes, since he can show that machines have them too.

And yet the really fundamental questions about mind, will, and consciousness are not to be disposed of so easily. D. M. MacKay, an eminent authority on artificial intelligence, has written:

. . . may I say that what impresses me more and more is the element of irreducible mystery that attends our human condition—a mystery which the fullest of physiological understanding would not dispel . . . the necessity for "mind talk" cannot be removed by any appeal to "brain talk", since no adequate substitute for it exists in these terms. In the end, in line with ancient wisdom, we have to face an irreducible dualism in our own nature—not, of necessity, a dualism of "stuffs", but a dualism of aspect which no mechanistic analysis can exhaust.[8]

This gives a partial answer to those who regard the cybernetic approach as reductionist. There is, however, another answer which seems to me equally important, and which is the one I am concerned with in this book. Its special feature is that it emerges from the very heart of the cybernetic approach itself.

The cybernetic explanation of behaviour is concerned with Plans. Now, a Plan, as I have pointed out, is a holon; it has component sub-Plans, and it is in turn a component of larger Plans. This means that one can ask two sorts of question about any Plan: how? and why? How? questions lead one downwards in the hierarchy, why? questions lead one upwards. If one asks how Man Bahadur could survive the Himalayan cold, the answer is to be found in the fineness of adjustment of his temperature control mechanism, but if one asks why he was there, the answer is to be found in a larger Plan—in this case, a religious one.

There is nothing accidental about the appearance of religion here. With fair accuracy, one could say that science is concerned with how, and religion and metaphysics with why. That is, science is primarily concerned with analysing, religion and metaphysics with integrating. But this generalization really holds good only for nineteenth-century science. Cybernetics, though a scientific concept, leads in the direction of integration and purpose, and so points to an eventual reconciliation between science and religion. It may seem surprising to find science and religion linked in this way, yet I believe that such a linkage is the logical outcome of the cybernetic revolution, and hence I tend to agree with Gregory Bateson's estimate of the importance of cybernetics which I quoted at the beginning of this chapter.

The Structure of Thinking

IN THE LAST chapter, I suggested that we think of the brain as storing Plans hierarchically. I now want to relate that idea of a functional hierarchy to the anatomical hierarchy which I described in Chapter Five, and on this basis to put forward an evolutionary description of thinking.

People who try to describe the difference between human and animal behaviour usually find themselves using words like "intelligence", "spontaneity", and "insight". When we see an animal performing an apparently purposive act, we often ask whether it was due to intelligence or instinct.* Intelligence implies reflection, insight, and thinking; instinct suggests invariability, rigidity. The distinction is no doubt crude, but it does seem to correspond to a genuine difference in degree if not in kind. And in fact if we look at the way the brain is built we do seem to find this difference represented in structural terms.

1. The lowest level in the brain hierarchy is that of the stem. Here, in the part known as the medulla oblongata, at the top of the spinal cord, we find groups of cells concerned with one of the most basic of biological rhythms—breathing. These cells constitute a breathing "centre", and, in some animals at least, it is possible to isolate sub-groups of cells concerned respectively with breathing in and breathing out. Stimulation of one group causes the animal to inhale, stimulation of the other causes it to exhale. The two groups are interconnected, so that they act reciprocally.

This arrangement lends itself perfectly to analysis as embodying a Plan for breathing. Like every other physiological Plan, of course, the breathing Plan is a holon; it forms part of the larger activities of the organism. The breathing centre is

* At least, we do if we are not professional psychologists. Most psychologists today prefer to talk of "drives", a term which sounds more decently mechanistic; however, drive and instinct seem to mean much the same thing.

influenced by various characteristics of the blood flowing through it (temperature, carbon dioxide content, and so on), and it is "wired up" to other parts of the brain. In this way, breathing rate and rhythm can alter in sleep, exercise, and other circumstances according to the needs of the body; and of course emotion affects it too, which is why the bosoms of Victorian heroines invariably heaved in moments of excitement, pleasurable or otherwise.

2. Moving up the hierarchy to the hypothalamus, we find that centres apparently exist which control much more complex plans. I have already mentioned that if the blood flowing through the hypothalamus is cooled, the animal starts to increase its heat production by shivering and so forth. But that is not all; it also starts to eat. Similarly, if the blood flowing through the hypothalamus is warmed, the animal starts to drink. In other words, the hypothalamic plan for temperature regulation involves elements of behaviour.

And there is more to the hypothalamus than that. It seems to control many different kinds of behaviour which are not directly related to the internal environment at all. This has become evident in the last 30 years or so, as the result of experiments in which the hypothalamus of animals has been stimulated directly, while the animals were going about their ordinary business. It is now possible to insert into the brain fine wires through which electric currents can be passed; alternatively, fine glass tubes are used and chemical substances introduced. Such techniques allow the selective stimulation of small brain areas, and they have yielded some surprising results.

For example, in cats it is fairly easy to obtain attack sequences, complete with erection of hair, lashing of tail, dilatation of pupils, scratching, biting, and so on.[1] In rats an even more surprising sequence can be produced; the animals will, in response to stimulation, pick up small objects such as pieces of wood and carry them from one part of their cage to another, continuing to do this as long as the current flows. In their natural state rats build nests, and presumably the carrying behaviour would be useful for this activity; guinea pigs, which do not build nests, do not show their behaviour in response to stimulation.[2]

It is almost as if the hypothalamus had a library of tapes, with instructions for performing various commonly used routines, which could be played by a touch on an appropriate button or "centre". That is, the hypothalamus apparently contains Plans which, when set going either by direct stimulation or as part of the natural processes within the brain, tend to run themselves off according to a preset schedule.*

A characteristic feature of these centres is that they seem to be analogous to homeostats. For example, if the drinking centre is stimulated with a given intensity of current, the animal does not go on drinking indefinitely. Instead, it takes a definite number of swallows and then stops. The effect of stimulation seems to be to reset the mechanism to a different level, so that the animal starts its drinking at a level of satiety which would not ordinarily cause it to drink. This is very much like setting the thermostat of a boiler to a higher value, so that the boiler goes on and off at a higher level than previously.[3]

Is it possible that "instincts" are mechanisms of this kind? Animal ethologists have described many examples of behaviour sequences which are triggered by specific stimuli. There are the mating rituals of many species of birds, the "rules" of fighting among mammals which usually prevent the victor from killing or seriously injuring the vanquished, and innumerable other types of behaviour all of which lend themselves very well to analysis in terms of Plan hierarchies and all of which, presumably, are controlled by centres in the brain core. The rôle of the specific stimulus—the mating colour of the male stickleback, or whatever it may be—is to trigger a mechanism. Electrical stimulation of the centre triggers it artificially.

Let me take another example. It is natural for domestic fowl to threaten hostile animals, such as weasels. The appropriate sequence of actions can be elicited by electrical stimulation of the fowl's brain.[4] If the bird is shown a stuffed weasel (the current not yet on) she will threaten the enemy. As the current is turned on and gradually increased, she becomes fiercer and eventually launches a full-scale attack. But what is very interesting is that, if the current continues to flow, she does not persist with the attack but instead breaks it off and

* Whether the hypothalamus really contains "centres" governing various forms of behaviour is still open to dispute, but this is currently the most widely accepted hypothesis. For a good discussion of the question, see Stellar, E., "The Physiology of Motivation"; in Bindra, D., and Stewart, J., 1971, pp. 395–403.

runs away, squawking loudly. This, of course, is the appropriate course of action in such a situation, because a weasel which stood its ground in the face of an attack would be a very dangerous enemy.

Hence, by stimulating the fowl's brain continuously one can elicit a complete and appropriate action sequence.

Another interesting point is that if a neutral object, such as a fist, is substituted for the stuffed weasel, the fowl will not attack it unless a stronger current is used. This suggests that the individual circumstances play a part in deciding what behavioural result will be produced by any given strength of current; response is not an all-or-nothing affair, but is in part influenced by the environment.

Instincts are usually thought of as inherited. However, there is no hard and fast dividing line between learned and inherited patterns of behaviour. The songs of birds, for instance, are partly learned and partly inherited, the exact proportions of the mixture varying from species to species. The tree pipit learns nothing; its song is wholly inherited. The linnet, on the other hand, learns everything; linnets will learn the song of almost any kind of bird they are reared with. Between these two extremes we find the chaffinch, which was the subject of some interesting experiments by Holger Poulsen in Denmark.[5]

Poulsen reared some young male chaffinches in isolation. Now, in Denmark the chaffinch begins to sing about mid-February. By the middle of January the young chaffinches were producing a rough and ready version of the chaffinch song, but it was quite imperfect. In mid-February Poulsen allowed his subjects to hear linnets singing. The chaffinches imitated the linnets as best they could, but with only moderate success. But as soon as they heard a chaffinch, they began to sing perfect chaffinch songs, and never imitated a linnet again.

We must assume that song patterns—song Plans—are built into the brains of birds with varying degrees of completeness. In the tree pipit the pattern is preformed entirely; all that is needed to trigger it is the right time of year. The linnet, on the other hand, inherits only a rudimentary impulse to sing, and the form of the song is decided from outside.

3. At the human level, very little behaviour, if any, is instinctive in the sense of being built in like the tree pipit's song; almost everything is learned, although there may perhaps be

underlying guide lines built into the structure of the brain which channel learning in particular directions; this idea seems to be implied by Noam Chomsky's theories about language.

But even though we have to learn our behaviour patterns, once they have been learned they can become very largely automatic. Most of the things we do every day—tying our shoelaces, signing our name, driving a car—are habitual actions, which have presumably been built into the brain through practice. There are two interesting points to notice about this.

The first is that habitual actions of this kind are very hard to eradicate, as nail-biters and smokers know, and even to modify them is difficult, which is why handwriting is so hard to disguise and why faulty techniques of playing musical instruments take a long time to correct.

The second point is that habitual actions often seem to be recorded in quite a general way. For example, you can write with a pen on paper, or with a piece of chalk on a blackboard, or even with your toe in the sand; in each case the muscles you are using are quite different, yet your handwriting will always be characteristic of you. This must mean that the Plan for handwriting is stored at quite a high level in the hierarchy.

It would be satisfying if one could point to some area of the brain and say that this is where automatic actions are recorded. Unfortunately, our ignorance is too great to allow us to do this. They may be recorded in the cortex, or they may be recorded in structures below the cortex, such as the basal nuclei. These are large masses of nerve cells deep inside the brain; Pribram has called them a "brain within a brain". They are clearly of evolutionary importance, because they are prominent in all mammals and birds; and there is actually some evidence that —in pigeons at least—they store learned actions.[6] Perhaps they do so in man too; but here one is frankly guessing.

It may be, indeed, that we should not look for any single anatomical area in which learned actions are stored as in a vast tape library; perhaps many areas of the brain collaborate in this. However, from the point of view of function, we are entitled to look on learned automatic actions as forming a grade in the hierarchy above that of purely instinctive actions. A motor skill, like driving or typing, is fixed, but only relatively so; it can, to a greater or lesser extent, be modified according to needs. For example, if you want to type in French instead of English you can do so, but—unless you are used to it—you will type more slowly in French, because you will not be using the constantly recurring English letter-sequences such as th-. But learned automatic actions are only relatively fixed; they can, to a greater or lesser extent, be modified according to need. There is no sharp cut-off between "closed" and "open" Plans; they shade off into one another imperceptibly.

The ability to change one's Plans, to be flexible—in a word, to learn—is the hallmark of evolution. It is chiefly in this sense that a dog is more evolved than a mouse, a chimpanzee more evolved than a dog, and a human being more evolved than a chimpanzee. This brings us to the fourth, and highest, level of the hierarchy.

4. The final level of the hierarchy is the cortex, which is the level of learning and change. All animals can learn to some extent, but really effective learning demands a well-developed brain, and especially a cortex, and hence is largely confined to birds and mammals. It is thanks to our large and elaborate cortex that we are able to change our behaviour patterns more freely than any other animal. It is chiefly in the cortex that new organization occurs, new "information" is generated.

The cortex, in fact, is the site where Plans are changed. At lower levels in the hierarchy we find the *results* of change recorded in the form of instinctive and other more or less automatic actions; at the cortical level we have the mechanism which permits change to occur. We are all aware of what this process of change feels like: it is what we call "thinking". Developing a sophisticated cortex endows organisms with the power of thinking. But on this view of the matter, it is not only human beings who ought to be able to think; other vertebrates too—at any rate the higher mammals—have pretty good brains, even if they are not so large and complex as our own, and thinking ought therefore to be found quite a long way down the evolutionary tree.

What does the study of animal behaviour tell us about this? In the first place, it shows quite conclusively, I believe, that the higher mammals at least do show evidence of "insight"; their actions are by no means wholly instinctive or even based on trial and error. Animals do think. I shall give some evidence of this in a moment, when I come to consider one of Wolfgang Köhler's experiments; anyone who wants more evidence should read Köhler's book and also the comprehensive survey by W. H. Thorpe mentioned in the bibliography.

There is also a second lesson to be learned from studies of animal behaviour. This is that the thinking process seems to depend on, and perhaps in the end to be identical with, the development of the ability to *make a mental "image" of the world*. Thus, Thorpe has emphasized the importance of the acquisition of the ability to keep something in mind when it is out of sight.

The lower mammals, it seems, lack this ability almost entirely. A female hamster, for instance, will protect her offspring while they are in the nest but may well eat them if she meets them outside. Similarly, a human baby takes some weeks to learn that a toy which has disappeared under a fold of the blanket is still there.

Hamster and baby both suffer from the same disability; they cannot keep two ideas in the mind simultaneously. As Thorpe puts it (my italics):

> I imagine that the animal's recognition of the continuance of an external world developed, at least in the animals and birds, *pari passu* with the ability to solve new problems by conscious insight. That is to say, as soon as the animal was in a position to produce a new solution to an unfamiliar problem, without trial-and-error behaviour, but by *a process of making a mental comparison and selection between possible alternatives based upon the relations which had been perceived*—as soon as it could do this, then it could begin to see the existence and coherence of a real world. So I think that, in animals as in men, the appreciation of reality, as distinct from the rest of experience, must be through its coherence and lawfulness.[7]

Notice particularly the phrase which I have italicized. This process of "mental comparison and selection between possible alternatives" is how mental development occurs, and it is the essence of *thinking*. Thinking, in fact, is almost synonymous with *imag*ination—the mental re-presentation of the world. On this view, thinking does not necessarily depend on language, and it becomes perfectly reasonable to say that animals other than man "think".

Perhaps the best known and most interesting of all studies

of thinking in animals is the classic work of Wolfgang Köhler
on chimpanzees. Köhler gave his animals many kinds of
problems to solve. For example, to obtain food they liked,
such as bananas, the chimpanzees had to pile boxes on top of
one another, or to use sticks; sometimes the sticks were not long
enough but could be made so by joining them together. Anyone
who reads Köhler's fascinating book *The Mentality of Apes*
without prejudice will, I think, agree with its author that the
animals often showed genuine insight and did not solve the
problems merely by chance or trial and error.

As an example, take what happened when one of Köhler's
most intelligent animals, Sultan, who had already succeeded
in fitting two tubes together so as to make a longer implement,
was confronted with a tube having a large opening and with a
narrow board which was just too wide to fit into the tube.[8]
After trying to fit the board into the tube and failing, Sultan
bit a splinter out of the side of the tube—a reasonable thing to
do, Köhler believes, because the side of the tube was in the way
of the board. Surprisingly, however, Sultan then tried to fit
this splinter into the opposite (unchewed) end of the tube, but
it was too big. He therefore went back to the board, and
narrowed it by biting it until it would go about two centi-
metres into the tube. However, this was not far enough, and
the board kept falling out of the tube. Becoming bored with this,
Sultan reverted to the splinter, and after sharpening it managed
to fit it into the sound end of the tube; thus he eventually
constructed the tool satisfactorily and reached the fruit.

In reading this account, one cannot reasonably avoid the
conclusion that Sultan had a purpose in mind—fitting the
two pieces of wood together to reach the fruit—and kept trying
out various ways of achieving his end until he found one that
worked. For Sultan, this problem-solving was quickly trans-
ferred from the mental level to the physical; he thought of a
solution, and at once tried it out. The difference between human
thinking and chimpanzee thinking seems to be, at least in
part, a question of "interiorization"; human beings can do a
good deal more "in their heads". Thus we come back to
*imag*ination; human beings have more mental images.

We could say, in fact, that images are the currency of
thought. Thinking consists in the mental manipulation of
images. A lowly animal, like a rat, solves most if not all of its

problems by trial and error. A chimpanzee, on the other hand, does not have to solve every problem in this way; instead, it can represent various courses of action to itself mentally and try them out beforehand, before committing itself to action. A human being designing a bridge or even writing a poem or a symphony is doing very much the same thing as the chimpanzee though at a very different level of complexity; and of course human beings often draw diagrams, scribble notes, or even make models to help their brains to manipulate the images they use.

Thought, I am suggesting, occurs in response to a challenge. When you encounter an unfamiliar situation, you search through your memory store for some pattern which corresponds and supplies a "solution". If you find one, well and good; you put it into effect. If not, you try to combine the various patterns available to you into some new composite pattern which will supply a solution. This is just what Sultan was trying to do.

Images and the Brain

We thus reach the conclusion that the function of the cortex is to produce images for the brain to manipulate, and this manipulation is thinking. But is there any evidence that the brain really does contain anything which corresponds to an image? This is still a violently contentious question, on which the experts disagree profoundly. In the last few years, however, a great deal of excitement has been generated by work on holography, and a number of people have speculated that the holographic principle might be the basis of images and memory.[9]

A hologram is in some ways like a photograph, but in others quite different. A photograph is obtained by placing a light-sensitive film in the image plane of a lens. A hologram, on the other hand, is obtained by placing the film in front of the image plane (in the focal plane) of the lens, the object meanwhile being illuminated by a "coherent" light source (a laser beam).

The resultant film, when it is developed, does not look anything like the original object. Instead of the object, all you see is a pattern of wave forms, something like a blurred fingerprint; this is actually a record of the wave patterns of light that were reflected by the object.

If, however, you illuminate the hologram suitably with a laser beam, the object becomes visible. But, unlike a photograph, the hologram shows the original scene in depth. If you move your head, the objects move relative to one another exactly as they would if you were really viewing them; perspective is preserved. Moreover, if you snip off one corner of the hologram and illuminate that, the *whole* of the original scene is reconstituted, even if not quite as sharply. This is because information about any single point on the original object is distributed evenly throughout the hologram. The hologram is thus resistant to damage.

The parallels between holography and memory will now, I think, begin to be evident. Memory is apparently widely distributed throughout the brain; this has been known since the classic experiments of K. S. Lashley, who showed that it is impossible to destroy memory provided one leaves any cortex behind at all. A further similarity comes from the potential richness of the holographic record. It is possible to superimpose several images on top of one another by making the holograms in a solid; each image is present throughout the solid, yet each can be extracted separately. Some ten thousand million items (bits) of information have been usefully stored in a cubic centimetre. This kind of feat affords a possible basis for conceiving a mechanism to account for the fantastic richness of memory—which is otherwise very difficult to account for.

In suggesting that the images which the brain uses may be holograms, I do not mean to imply that all our thinking is necessarily visual. "Image" is a general term. No doubt most of our images are chiefly visual (except, of course, in the case of people born blind), but there are also auditory, tactile, and kinaesthetic images, and there are images which are made up of combinations of these modalities. Most people seem to think predominantly in particular modalities, although it seems possible to extend one's range with practice. There are a few people who deny using any images at all when they think, but I suspect that they really do use images of some kind or other without realizing it; not everyone, for example, would recognize a kinaesthetic image as an image. (To experience a kinaesthetic image, try to remember which shoe you habitually put on first.) People who deny that they use images when they think would be something like those who deny that they dream;

modern research has shown that seemingly everyone does dream for about a quarter of every night, and people who deny that they dream have merely forgotten their dreams.

Images and Plans

There is a close relationship between images and Plans. Thus, a kinaesthetic image of what it feels like to write, or use a screwdriver, or swim is also a Plan for doing each of these things. It may well be that images and Plans are really much the same thing—holographic patterns—in different parts of the brain. In the front (motor) part they would be Plans, in the rear (sensory) part they would be images. If this idea is anywhere near correct, thought would depend on an interplay between motor and sensory parts of the brain via the deep (core) structures, and would result in the building up and elaboration of new images and Plans. Pribram describes thinking like this.

> Thought, as search, is initiated (by the posterior mechanism of the brain) when a mismatch between input and memory is not resolved through action. Thought is maintained (by the frontolimbic mechanism) until a more or less preset criterion for what is considered a match is met.[10]

It is currently fashionable for governments to commission military strategists and other planners to "simulate" various situations—diplomatic confrontations, wars, and so on—to see what might happen in real life. The experience so gained, will, it is hoped, increase the flexibility and subtlety of the government's response in an actual crisis.

I think we could picture the cortex as fulfilling this kind of rôle for the brain. It forms a vast reservoir of images (memories) and plans, which interact as thought. And our actions emerge from this interplay.*

---

* On this view, an essential part of thinking consists in making comparisons. There is some evidence, still incomplete, that the hippocampus (usually regarded as forming part of the limbic system) is concerned with comparison and learning.

Thinking and the Cycle of Differentiation

The hypothesis about thinking which I have put forward in this chapter is closely related to the concept of the cycle of differentiation. Indeed, it is the cycle of differentiation under another name. For the process of elaboration of images and Plans is also one of differentiation, and serves to increase the fineness with which behaviour is adjusted to circumstances. This idea will underlie my whole discussion of TM in the following Part. (If you are not yet practising TM, you will probably find it helpful at this point to re-read quickly through Chapter Two again before continuing.)

PART THREE

VIII

The Mechanism of TM

ANYONE WHO HAS borne with me throughout the last few chapters will, I expect, already have guessed the outline of the theory about TM which I want to put forward. In essence, my idea is as follows.

The brain is constantly trying to gain balance, through the cycle of differentiation, and this searching for balance is what we experience as thinking. *TM is a technique for facilitating the gaining of balance. During a TM period, therefore, the cycle of differentiation is revolving especially rapidly, and this leads to evolution.*

Anyone, whether he is a meditator or not, who sits down and does nothing in particular will of course "think"—that is, his brain will attempt to reach equilibrium. This process will be experienced as the "stream of consciousness"—the continuous procession of ideas, words, and images which drift across the mind so long as we are awake, and, indeed, also for much of the time we are asleep. Ordinarily, such thinking is more or less "gross"—on the surface of the mind, although some small "dips" do occur. (Such spontaneous dips are the basis of the "flash of inspiration", as I shall explain in a later chapter.) The effect of introducing TM into this situation is to deepen the dips, or—to put it differently—to facilitate the organizing capacity of the brain.

Probably the "vibrational" effects of the mantra are important here. There is nothing occult about this idea. What I have in mind is something analogous to the "Chladni effect", discovered in the eighteenth century by the German physicist Ernst Chladni and studied in detail in our own time by the Swiss Hans Jenny.[1]

Chladni showed that if sand is scattered on a vibrating metal plate all sorts of interesting patterns emerge. These are often "organic", resembling the concentric rings on a tree trunk, the hexagonal network of a honeycomb, or the spiral of a shell.

Many people have speculated on the idea that these resemblances are not accidental but reflect regularities inherent in the nature of the cosmos which have a decisive influence on the way life develops.

At a simple level, this is undoubtedly true. For example, virus particles inside cells are often not scattered haphazardly but arrange themselves into regular crystal-like polyhedrons. It is true that viruses are very elementary forms of life—indeed, they are on the borderline between life and non-life—and so perhaps it is not surprising that they should find themselves constrained by the requirements of simple geometry. But even complex animals have only a very few basic symmetries: spherical, found in certain protozoa; radial, as in starfish; and bilateral, as in ourselves. It may be that more complex, less readily apparent, regularities underlie all manifestations of life. (The physicist Erwin Schrödinger described the chromosome as an "aperiodic crystal".) Perhaps cymatics, as Jenny calls his subject, may have something important to tell us about the development of embryos and other complex biological processes, including the behaviour of the brain. If so, the ancient Indian belief in the power of mantras to produce specific effects on the minds of those who use them correctly would receive remarkable confirmation.

At any rate, my hypothesis is that, during TM, there occur changes in the way the cortex is organized which tend to bring about balance within the brain. The effect of TM, I believe, is to facilitate the *natural* tendency of the cortex to differentiate itself and so to refine the tuning of the brain. The natural goal of the brain is balance, and thinking is the subjective reflection of the balancing process. TM does not introduce a new principle; rather, it takes advantage of the fundamental principle on which the nervous system works.

If this idea is right, TM will necessarily have a cyclical or wave-like character. One sits down and starts the process; the brain moves towards balance. When balancing has gone as far as it can at the moment, a point of temporary equilibrium is reached. But—as a rule, anyway—this equilibrium will not be complete. Some activity is still going on; more or less fine cortical perturbations are still occurring. But just because the over-all level of activity has fallen somewhat, any fine perturbations which may still be present will have more influence than they did when the system was more unstable, as at the beginning of meditation. It is as if a roomful of chattering people had suddenly fallen silent, allowing a whispered conversation to become suddenly audible for the first time. To put it differently, the improvement in balance has simultaneously caused an increase in sensitivity.

Now the cycle starts to repeat itself. New sensitivity leads to new reorganization and differentiation, a new point of balance is reached, and so on. The logical end-point of this process is a condition where *all* on-going activity has been damped down by the refining process and balance is, at least for the present, perfect. This is restful alertness.

The psychological experience of a "typical" TM period (but please remember that this is only a theoretical description and is *not* to be taken as a norm) fits in very well, as you will see, with the concept of the cycle of differentiation. My hypothesis is that we can regard TM as a technique for increasing the efficiency of the cycle of differentiation.

TM and the Experience of Happiness

We saw in Chapter Two that happiness supplies the motive power for transcending. What draws the attention downwards, towards ever subtler regions of experience, is experience of increasing happiness. Now, why should this be? In Chapter Two I merely gave it as something which in practice is found to be so, but now I should like to try to account for it in terms of what we know about the brain.

The clue is to be found in our own experience of what it is to be alive. Have you ever climbed for hours under a blazing sun, becoming more and more hot, parched, and ravenous as the hours passed, and then arrived at last at a pool in the shade of a willow grove where you could drink your fill, plunge into cool water, and eat your sandwiches? If so, you will know that no sybarite, no gourmet, has experienced happiness anywhere near equal to yours at this moment.

What is the explanation? What happens in the brain when one is hot, hungry, or thirsty, and these deviations from normality are suddenly corrected? And why should correction cause happiness?

As for what happens in the brain, we already know the

answer, at least in outline. All these deviations concern the regulation of the internal environment, and so are registered by the various regulating centres in the hypothalamus. The converse situation—coming into a warm room after walking for miles in the teeth of a bitter north-east gale with snow on it, for example—also yields intense happiness, and the same principle applies here. Disturbance of the internal environment is registered by the core homeostats in the hypothalamus, which then try to compensate for the disturbance by switching on the appropriate regulating mechanisms—heat loss or heat production, eating, drinking, or whatever is required. At the same time, *severe or prolonged imbalance of a homeostat causes distress or unhappiness, and restoration of balance causes happiness.*

There is some interesting and important experimental evidence which sheds light on this idea. In 1954 two researchers at McGill University, James Olds and Peter Milner, were studying the behaviour of rats which had had electrodes implanted in (as Olds and Milner supposed) the reticular formation of the brain. By mistake, however, they had put the electrodes too far forward, and so they made, by accident, one of the most surprising discoveries about the brain to be reported so far in this century.

What they found was that the rat apparently enjoyed the electrical stimulus, for each time the current was turned on it would run to the same part of its cage—the spot where it had been when it first received the stimulus. Olds and Milner therefore provided it with a lever which it could press to stimulate its own brain, and as soon as it learned how to do so it spent many apparently happy hours at the task.[2]

Since that first discovery, the experiment has been repeated many times, and has led to the mapping of a number of "reward" areas in the brain core. Such areas have been shown to exist in man as well as rats; when they are stimulated, patients become more alert and bright, so that depression can be converted almost instantaneously into euphoria and relief from intense physical pain can be obtained.[3] Some researchers have not hesitated to claim that such experiments have revealed the "pleasure areas" of the brain, and a few have gone on to postulate that all human activity can be interpreted as an attempt to stimulate these areas through natural channels.[4]

Pribram has put forward a more restrained and, to me, more

appealing view. He suggests that when the brain core mechanisms are stimulated the receptors for hunger, thirst, and so on are reset "so that the organism does in fact have the feeling of being temporarily hungry, thirsty, and the like and then quickly feels momentarily satiety only to repeat the cycle once more".[5] Hence the animal experiences constantly recurring moments of happiness as the core homeostats continually return to balance. Pribram compares self-stimulation to repeatedly turning the central heating on and off by twisting the dial on the thermostat.

From an evolutionary point of view, it obviously makes sense that upsetting the internal environment should cause unhappiness and restoring it to normality should cause happiness; this is what we should expect. And this, I believe, is the explanation for the happiness experienced during TM.

I do not mean to say that *all* human happiness is related to the state of the core homeostats, nor do I mean to say that the happiness experienced during TM is wholly related to these structures; it is the principle I want to draw attention to. Even so far as basic experiences such as hunger and thirst are concerned, the real state of affairs is a good deal more complicated than my thumbnail sketch suggests. It makes a good deal of difference, for example, whether you are climbing a mountain for pleasure or because you are escaping from pursuers. Nevertheless, the state of the internal environment is a most important element in one's state of mind, a fact which "civilized" people tend to forget: it is difficult (though perhaps not impossible) to be happy when one is cold or hungry.

My thesis is that what determines one's state of happiness or unhappiness at any given moment is the over-all balance of the brain. This does not contradict the idea that all the various brain areas may perhaps concentrate their influence on one central controlling site, such as the hypothalamus or limbic system, but what is paramount is balance. My main assumption in this book is that the *whole* brain is built up of interlocking feedback structures, and that the concept of balance can thus be applied to all the brain areas and also to the brain as a whole. At any given moment, some areas will be in balance, others will not. The more of the brain that is out of balance, the greater will be the sense of unrest and even unhappiness. Coming back to balance, conversely, will cause happiness. If *all* the brain homeostats could come into balance simultaneously, the result would presumably be an experience of "total" happiness, greater than could be achieved in any other way. On my hypothesis, this is what happens in the state of restful alertness.

Maharishi has made the interesting point that it is the instant of *contact* with pure awareness—the moment when restful alertness is first gained—which is experienced as perfect happiness.[6] Once one has become as it were totally immersed in and fused with pure awareness there can be no more experience of happiness because the subject-object relation has ceased to exist, whereas for happiness to be experienced there must be an experiencer and also something to be experienced. This idea fits in perfectly with the homeostatic theory. One knows from experience that it is the *first* draught of water when one is thirsty, the *first* mouthful of food when one is ravenous, which gives the most intense happiness. Gradually, over the succeeding minutes, the happiness dies away until it is no longer perceptible. In other words, the happiness which results from restoration of a disturbed homeostat to normal occurs at the moment of *change*.

Stress and Stress Resolution

Just as restoration of balance creates happiness, so prolonged or severe deviation from balance leads to discomfort or unhappiness. Here, I believe, we have a physiological explanation for stress. In terms of my theory, *stress is a failure of the brain to achieve balance.*

Just now I used the example of the way the core homeostats control the internal environment to illustrate what imbalance feels like, but the kind of imbalance I think of as important in relationship to TM is at a higher level in the brain hierarchy. Stress in the TM sense is probably recorded mainly in the cortex, and is connected with our experience of the outer world.

Perhaps I could illustrate my meaning by referring to a classic case described by Wilder Penfield.[7] A girl of fourteen was operated on for epilepsy. Her attacks were invariably preceded by a hallucination, in which she saw herself in a scene which had actually occurred. At the age of seven she had been walking through a field with her brothers when a man came up behind her and said: "How would you like to get into this bag with the snakes?" She screamed with fright and together with her brothers ran home, where she told her mother about the event. Subsequently she suffered from nightmares during which she lived through the episodes, and when, at the age of eleven, she began to suffer from epilepsy, the scene, as I have said, recurred in her mind with great vividness, so that she seemed to herself to be in two places at once.

At operation, Penfield found that electrical stimulation of the cortex of the temporal lobe reproduced her hallucination. Moreover, if the electrode was kept in place on the cortex, the memory unfolded itself in sequence, like a film. The cause of her epileptic attacks was found to be an area of brain damage which she had apparently sustained as an infant, when she was given an anaesthetic. Scarring had developed over the years, and had given rise to the fits. But why should they be preceded by the vivid memory of the fright she had received at the age of seven? Penfield believes that the damaged area was "triggering" the memory which had been formed at the time of the experience, and which he was also able to trigger with his electrode.

In this case, we have direct experimental evidence of a severe stress having been recorded in the cortex. Admittedly the picture is complicated by the epilepsy caused by the earlier brain damage, but even if there had been no brain damage the experience would still have been recorded and might well have given rise to nightmares and other behavioural disturbances, as frequently happens with any psychologically traumatic experience. The brain damage is in a sense irrelevant; it led to the operation, and hence to Penfield's discovery, but it brings into view a much more general aspect of brain function. (Penfield removed the damaged area of brain, including the part of the cortex from which he had elicited the memory, but although the fits ceased the memory was not eradicated, so it must have been recorded somewhere else as well—perhaps in the other temporal lobe.)

My hypothesis is that stresses of this general kind are present in all our brains, and interfere to a greater or lesser extent in the smooth functioning of the whole. Whenever a lasting cortical disturbance is set up it remains as a potential source of disturbance, like a piece of grit in a machine. Notice that it need not be active all the time, just as the memory of the frightening experience was not constantly present in the mind of Penfield's patient. Many stresses, no doubt, are latent, and only become active when they are triggered by some chance configuration of cortical patterns. Indeed, as Freud emphasized, it is not necessary for a "conflict" to be present in awareness if it is to produce effects; it may disturb smooth functioning without producing any actual memory. This may be the basis of an obsession—an idea which cannot be expelled from the mind, or a compulsion to perform a useless action, such as checking that the front door is locked although one knows perfectly well that it is. Another effect may be useless worry which continues even though all possible steps in a given situation have been taken. The impossibility of reasoning such symptoms away will be familiar to everyone. If, as I have suggested, they are due to imbalances in the brain it is easy to see why simply willing them to disappear is so futile. The attack must be physical.

If the idea which I put forward in the last chapter—that the brain really contains images in some form—is correct, many forms of stress in human beings might be due to a conflict between incompatible images. For example, you are looking for an ideal wife, and cannot make up your mind whether to propose to Mary or Jane. Both ladies have some of the features of your ideal, but not all; hence in each case there is a discrepancy between the actual and the ideal, and your mind will be filled with thoughts related to this—that is, you "turn the matter over in your mind" (a most significant metaphor, this) as you try the fit of each lady in turn to your image of perfection.

Resolution of the conflict can come in a number of ways. You may change your ideal. You may decide to marry Jane and leave Mary, or vice versa; you may marry Jane but keep up a relationship with Mary; or you may marry neither. Any of these solutions may satisfy you. It may be, however, that resolution is incomplete; you marry Jane, but feel regret about Mary, or you carry on a clandestine relationship with Mary and feel guilty about it. In all these cases conflict continues and is a source of stress.

Notice that if resolution *is* achieved, it is by constructing a new, more comprehensive, image, which transcends the original conflict. It is not that the conflict is forgotten and wiped out as if it has never existed. Even if you settle down happily with Jane and cease to feel any regrets about Mary, you will still remember her. In later years you will think back on the torments of indecision you suffered, but they will no longer affect you; it will be almost as if they had happened to someone else. And in a sense they did, because in resolving the conflict you have evolved; you have built up a new level of mental (and presumably physical) organization. Stress resolution is a hierarchical affair, and occurs through the cycle of differentiation.

This, I believe, is what happens during TM. When one "transcends", new organization occurs in the cortex, and this new organization exerts finer control on the general mechanism of the brain, increasing its stability and also its sensitivity. Admittedly this idea can be only a hypothesis at present, and indeed probably for a long time to come, but it does seem to me a reasonable one in the light of present knowledge. In the next chapter I shall be looking at some facts about the brain and its workings which seem to me to support the view I am putting forward here. At present, however, I want to take the implications of the fine tuning hypothesis a little further.

Fine Tuning and the Growth to Enlightenment

In Chapter Two, you will remember, I explained that, for Maharishi, gaining the state of restful alertness (corresponding to the experience of pure awareness) was not an end in itself but was a stage on the road to enlightenment. The next step in the process was to make pure awareness a permanent reality, and the way to do this was by continually alternating between the deep rest of meditation and the turmoil of activity.

This idea, we saw, is at variance with the conventional teaching about meditation. It is, however, very much what one would predict on the fine-tuning theory.

To recapitulate for a moment: the state of restful alertness occurs, I have suggested, when all the various homeostatic cycles in the brain have achieved balance. However, this state will initially be temporary, because all *possibility* of disturbance has not been eliminated.

During TM, the refining process is occurring on the basis of material already recorded in the brain; what is being reshuffled and organized is *existing* ideas (information). As soon as the meditator opens his eyes at the end of the meditation period, however, fresh information begins to pour in, and modifications begin anew in the structure and organization of the brain. The patterns which were built up in the meditation period are put to the test, are subjected to a sort of natural selection. The sensitivity of the system has been increased, and hence the circumstances are not the same as they were. After meditation, the world is perceived slightly differently.

The result is that the next time one sits down to meditate new conflicts, new stresses, have to be resolved. This does not mean that nothing was achieved at the previous sitting; on the contrary, just because some changes did occur the response of the system to the outer world is now different from what it was. Not only has the over-all amount of stress been reduced; its disposition has been altered. The effects of activity are to "shake the brain up", to change its configurations, and to give the cycle of differentiation fresh material upon which to work. One could perhaps compare the brain to a kaleidoscope, which is alternately shaken by activity and allowed to come to rest during meditation, when the results of shaking can be viewed. But, to complete the analogy, we must stipulate that the coloured fragments inside the kaleidoscope are changed after each shaking so that the pattern they make approximates more and more closely to an ideal. In other words, there is continual feedback between rest and activity.

Thus the total refinement cycle includes not merely the alternation between greater and lesser amounts of activity which occur *during* meditation, but also the larger alternation from meditation to activity and back again. As a result of the revolution of this larger cycle, the tuning of the nervous system becomes more and more perfect until, eventually, it reaches a point when it is in permanent balance. It seems to be this larger cycle of refinement which gives rise to a common experience of people who practise TM: there are times when one has a feeling of special well-being, and times when all one's perceptions are clouded, as if a layer of mud at the bottom of the mind had been stirred up. Over a long period, the trend is towards greater clarity of awareness, but this clarity develops in a cyclical fashion. It is in this way that the fifth state of awareness comes into being.

4*

Maharishi describes the fifth state as that in which the inner pure awareness of the transcendental (fourth) state is maintained together with the waking, dreaming, or deep sleep states. One of the principal characteristics of this state, as I mentioned in Chapter Three, is that in it experiences are said to be like a "line on water", vanishing almost as soon as they have been produced. How can we account for this on the fine tuning theory?

Surely it is just what one would expect. The fifth state is one in which the tuning of the brain has become so fine that incoming impressions fail to disturb the over-all balance and are accommodated as soon as they arrive.

Ordinarily there is a good deal of disturbance within the brain because the tuning and hence the stability are far from perfect. Stability can be gained temporarily during TM, and this is the state of pure awareness. The fifth state, permanent pure awareness, occurs when the system is so finely tuned that it can damp out disturbances as soon as they occur.

It is tempting to speculate that the mechanism which is chiefly concerned with the maintenance of permanent pure awareness is the brain stem and hypothalamus, which house the reticular activating system. This system, as I explained in Chapter Five, interacts with the higher brain centres such as the thalamus and cortex and plays a very important part in maintaining awareness. Now, Maharishi has always insisted that the inability to maintain permanent pure awareness at all times, in waking, dreaming, and deep sleep, is the result of faulty brain functioning. We *ought* to be in the fifth state. May it be that the reason we are not in this state is that stress centres in the cortex disturb the smooth functioning of the core mechanisms which maintain awareness, causing them to oscillate too widely? (Remember that there are important two-way —feedback—connections between the reticular formation and all parts of the cortex.)[8] Eliminating the stressed areas in the cortex would allow the basic core mechanisms to function more smoothly, and so to maintain awareness at all times in the manner which Maharishi describes.

Higher States of Consciousness
Even in a theoretical discussion like this, it is difficult to go

much beyond the fifth state of consciousness because to do so one must venture so far outside the boundaries of one's own experience. Nevertheless, for the sake of completeness I should like to sketch in—hesitantly—the way in which I think the concept of fine adjustment might be applied to these higher states.

The essence of further evolution after the fifth state has been gained lies, as I explained in Chapter Two, in *refinement of the mechanism of perception*. To account for this on the present theory one would have to assume that the mechanisms of perception are essentially based on cybernetic principles. I have already mentioned (in Chapter Six) that the nervous system contains filters, which are "set" by the brain so as to control the amount of information which is allowed to reach consciousness. Perception is thus active, not passive. Moreover, it now appears that the brain does not merely filter information, it actively modifies it. Thus Pribram tells us that there is now "good evidence that the so-called association areas of the cerebral cortex exert a type of control over the input systems which is in many respects similar to that exercised when a zoom lens is extended and retracted".[9]

I find this a most exciting notion. Pribram's picture of the brain is light-years away from the dull, static, telephone-exchange picture current in the early decades of this century. According to that picture, the eye was a camera and the brain merely a rather elaborate photographic film. Now we have the idea of the brain as dynamic, changing, building up its view of the world in an organic fashion. Probably each of us sees the world in a way which is different from that of everyone else; our vision may well be as personal and individual as our fingerprints. And the vision changes as the brain changes; truly, "knowledge is structured in consciousness".

These ideas seem to me to suggest the outlines of an understanding of the mechanisms which give rise to higher states of consciousness. The gaining of enlightenment, I suggest, depends on increasing the sophistication of the brain mechanisms which regulate perception so that the senses can reveal a more complete and accurate picture of the world. It is as if we were born as simple box cameras which could subsequently be modified, by the incorporation of new lenses, shutters, filters and so on until they became completely transformed into the most refined and advanced of modern cameras. According to SCI, our brains are like this; through the practice of TM, they can gradually evolve into supremely accurate and sensitive instruments. The Blakean vision which sees "a World in a grain of sand/And a Heaven in a wild flower" may well have a physiological foundation in the way the cortex influences perception.

Summary

I have suggested that the experience of TM and the way in which, according to Maharishi, evolution occurs through the practice of TM can be usefully described in terms of the cycle of differentiation. During TM, I believe, the brain is going through the various stages of the cycle and this is how it evolves to give rise, first to permanent Self-awareness, and later to full enlightenment on the perceptual level.

In this chapter I have limited myself to describing what I take to be the principle on which TM works. In the remainder of Part Three I shall look at the main implications of this approach.

Evidence and Implications

HOWEVER MUCH FUN a hypothesis may be—at least for the person who has thought it up—it ought to earn its keep. It ought to be supported by evidence and it ought also to have implications for future research—that is, it ought to be capable of being tested in some way to find out whether it is valid. What I want to do now is to say something about the fine tuning hypothesis from both points of view.

Broadly speaking, there are three ways in which one might look for evidence to support or refute a theory about how TM works. The first is to take account of what meditators say they experience. This I have already done—indeed, as I explained in Chapter Three, it was largely the subjective aspect of TM which led me to formulate the fine tuning hypothesis in the first place. From the subjective point of view, the evidence fits the theory, and this is important because in the present case subjective evidence does have value, however unfashionable it may be to say so. But other kinds of evidence are needed too.

The second line of attack is to investigate TM and its effects objectively, by means of physiological and psychological tests. This is of course the approach that carries most weight with scientists, and rightly so, but it suffers from the disadvantage that one cannot study the brain changes of meditators directly; all the methods that can be used are indirect. Moreover, in the nature of the case one cannot use animals, so in practice there are limits to what the objective approach can yield.

The third line of attack is more indirect still. It is to look at what has been discovered about the brain in other circumstances which resemble TM more or less closely, and to see how far the findings can shed light on TM.

In this chapter I want to consider TM from the second and third points of view.

Direct Evidence About TM

The experimental evidence about TM, although still preliminary, is so voluminous that I cannot hope to review it here. Instead, I want to concentrate on a few findings which seem to me specially important. I do not propose to say much about the metabolic effects described by Keith Wallace and Herbert Benson in their pioneer work,[1] because I think that the metabolic changes, interesting and important though they are, are secondary to the changes in the brain, and therefore it is to the brain that we must look if we are to understand what is happening in TM.

Unfortunately, the brain is very difficult to study. The only tool which has so far been applied to the brain in TM is the electroencephalograph (EEG). This is essentially an amplifier coupled to a recording device, and it is used to detect the minute fluctuations that occur in the electrical activity of the brain. The EEG is inevitably a crude instrument, since ordinarily it has to be applied to the surface of the scalp and thus is picking up the activity of the brain only through a fair thickness of tissue; similarly, it yields direct information only about the surface (cortex) of the brain. Moreover, the information it provides is derived from quite large areas of cortex and hence is somewhat imprecise. There are other difficulties as well; nevertheless, in the hands of experts the EEG has provided a vast amount of exciting information about what happens to the brain in different states. The EEG is an extraordinarily valuable tool; however, it is as well to remember that it is very far from providing a "God's eye" view of what is going on in the brain. As one EEG specialist remarked to me recently, EEG interpretation is more of an art than a science.

The usual technique is to record the activity at a number of sites on the scalp simultaneously, and then to analyse the tracings in various ways, often with the help of a computer. The tracings take the form of waves of various amplitudes and frequencies, and these are conventionally given the names of Greek letters—alpha, beta, and so on.

A great many frequencies can actually be recorded, but the faster ones are difficult to study and have therefore received little attention. The best-known patterns found in the waking state are the alpha rhythm (eight to twelve cycles per second), which is usually found towards the back of the head when the eyes are closed, tending to disappear if the eyes are opened or the subject is asked to perform mental arithmetic, and the beta rhythm (fourteen to twenty-five cycles per second), which is found in the forward parts of the head and seems to be associated with mental effort.

Not much has so far been published about the EEG findings during TM, although a great deal of research is currently under way and we may look forward to an immense outflowing of information shortly. The most interesting reports which have so far appeared are by Dr Jean-Paul Banquet.[2] According to him, the most characteristic and important feature of the EEG during meditation is a tendency towards orderliness and synchronization. This appears in various ways.

First, alpha activity, normally present at the back of the head, spreads forward to cover the whole of the brain. This happens at the beginning of meditation; later, there is a change from alpha to the slower theta frequency, which spreads in the opposite direction, from before backwards. In four of Banquet's fifteen subjects a third stage of meditation—subjectively reported as "deep"—occurred; this was characterized by predominant beta activity, which again tended to start at the front and work backwards. As the meditation period drew to an end, alpha rhythm reappeared. An interesting and unusual finding was that, in "advanced" meditators, alpha rhythm tended to persist when the subjects opened their eyes.

Banquet lays great emphasis on his finding of synchronization. First, synchronization occurred between the front and back of the brain; alpha, beta, or theta waves tended to spread over the whole brain. Second, synchronization occurred between the two hemispheres, left and right. These two features reflect topographical synchronization—synchronization between areas. But there is more to it than that. In addition, Banquet found, there was synchronization of the phases of the waves; the peaks were occurring in different brain areas, and even in both hemispheres, simultaneously. Sometimes even the shapes of the waves were similar in the various brain areas.

What do these findings mean? This is a difficult question, which is bound to occupy EEG specialists for a long time to come. Banquet himself has suggested that the synchronization of cortical activity reflects the setting up of a feedback loop between the cortex and deeper structures, such as the thalamus and hypothalamus. Banquet is impressed by the increasing "orderliness" of brain activity during TM. So, of course, am I, because it fits in very well with my hypothesis. If we assume, as I have done, that TM is a process of gaining balance, it would be logical to expect the EEG findings which Banquet describes. The state of restful alertness might very probably appear in the EEG as perfect cortical synchronization. I therefore find Banquet's work, so far as it goes, most interesting.

However, I do not mean to say more about the various findings, including the EEG ones, during TM, for two reasons. The first is the very preliminary nature of the research so far carried out. The work which has so far been done is suggestive and exciting, but until it has been repeated, verified, and amplified it will be unsafe to build any firm conclusions upon it.

The second reason is perhaps the more important of the two. It is that I think the most useful research so far carried out, and certainly the research which holds the greatest promise for the future, concerns not the TM state itself but the effects of TM on thought and activity outside meditation.

One would, I think, expect this to be so. During TM, the state of the brain must—if the "stress release" theory is right—be changing rapidly from moment to moment as the resolution of stresses proceeds. Thus there is no single TM state which can be isolated and studied, but rather a fairly rapid succession of states, which fluctuate from moment to moment during the meditation period. No doubt there will be short episodes of more or less complete "restful alertness", but these will usually be almost impossible to pick out by current physiological techniques. The EEG techniques which are used, for example, depend on computer averaging of wave forms over a period of time; they cannot detect very brief deviations from a prevailing rate or rhythm, yet such deviations might be the most significant features of all.

I believe it will be much easier and more informative to study the fairly long-term effects of TM, and this approach would also accord with the basic teaching about TM, which is, as I have emphasized, that one meditates not for the experience but for the effects. Some studies of the effects of TM have already been carried out, and many more are under way or have been planned. Here I should like to single out one or two which seem to me specially interesting in the light of the fine-tuning hypothesis.

The first was a pilot study carried out some years ago by Dr David Orme-Johnson at the University of Texas at El Paso.[3] The aim was to measure the way the body responds to stress. As the basis of measurement, Orme-Johnson used the change in the electrical resistance of the skin that occurs in response to stress. When a current is passed through the skin, it encounters a resistance which varies from time to time. Not much is known about why this is so or what the changes mean, although there is some suggestion that high values for skin resistance are linked with states of calmness and relaxation. ("Lie detectors" work, in part, by measuring falls in skin resistance found when an awkward question is asked.)

In Orme-Johnson's experiment, a group of meditators was subjected to a repeated sudden loud noise and the changes in skin resistance were recorded. A group of non-meditators was also studied for comparison. Orme-Johnson found definite differences between the times taken by the two groups to return to normal values of skin resistance each time the sound was made. In one typical study, the skin responses of the meditators had fallen almost to zero by about fifteen minutes, while those of the non-meditators fell much more slowly and were still quite perceptible after 40 minutes.

As I say, this was only a pilot study, and it cannot bear very much weight; I mention it mainly as an indication of the kind of research which, on my hypothesis, ought to give useful information.

Some very exciting recent work by Dr Denver Daniels, of the University of Exeter, also has relevance to my view of TM.[4] Daniels subjected his unfortunate subjects to the most unpleasant noises he could devise, such as a finger nail scraping on a blackboard, and then measured the time needed for the skin resistance to return to normal (much as in Orme-Johnson's experiment). Normal people take about five minutes to reach normality after a stress of this kind. Practitioners of TM returned to normal more quickly—within three minutes or less—and what was specially interesting was that subjects who had been meditating for about three years showed no fall in skin resistance at all *even though they felt distressed and showed it by grimacing and protesting.*

It is this last point which seems to me so remarkable. For, if it turns out to be true that TM does really eliminate the physiological response to stress while preserving the psychological aspect of the experience, we shall have found a beautiful experimental verification of Maharishi's "line on water" description of the effects of TM. And this would also fit in perfectly with the fine-tuning hypothesis, according to which the physiological response to stress is absent because it is "damped out" by the fine tuning mechanisms in the brain. I would predict that other studies of this general kind would support the idea that TM enhances "autonomic" stability, and it should not be too difficult to devise them.

For example, techniques have recently been developed for continuous (24-hour) recording of heart rate and rhythm, and also of the EEG, in people who are moving about and leading a normal life. Such techniques have already yielded some interesting results. Thus, it has been found that many people, when subjected to apparently mild stress, such as that of driving a car or making a speech, show sharp increases in heart rate, and at times the rhythm becomes abnormal as well. These changes could be dangerous in some people, and doctors have therefore given patients at risk in this way drugs which block the nerves that speed up the heart in response to excitement. This treatment is quite effective; it prevents the rise in heart rate in response to stress. Unfortunately, however, the drugs themselves can produce adverse effects if they are used for long periods, and also there may be other results of stress which are less easy to measure and which are not prevented by the drugs.

Clearly it would be much better if the speeding up of the heart, as well as the other effects of stress, could be prevented "naturally". TM may well do this. It would therefore be very interesting to apply these techniques for continuous measurement of heart rate, EEG, and so on to meditators, and see how, if at all, they differ from other people in their physiological response to life. On the fine-tuning hypothesis, one could expect them to respond to stress only briefly, and probably less dramatically than non-meditators.

There are, of course, immense possibilities for research into the possible effects of TM as a long-term preventer of various diseases, such as high blood pressure, coronary heart disease, and so on, and all these are linked indirectly to the fine-tuning hypothesis. But here I want to confine myself to reasonably direct forms of investigation, and the ideas I have mentioned will give an indication of the areas which at present seem to me to be worth exploring.

So far, the examples of improved efficiency through fine tuning which I have given have been mostly concerned with the autonomic (involuntary) nervous system, which controls such functions as heart rate, skin resistance, and so on. However, there is also the interesting possibility that TM improves "motor performance" (voluntary activity) as well. It is worth looking at this idea for a moment, because it has important philosophical overtones.

An important characteristic of Maharishi's concept of enlightenment is that it leads to "skill in action". The *Bhagavad Gita* says "Yoga is skill in action". Maharishi comments on this as follows:

> What is skill in action? It is the technique of performing action so that the whole process becomes easy. The action is completed with the least effort, leaving the doer fresh enough to enjoy fully the fruits of his action while at the same time remaining untouched by its binding influence.[5]

Usually, I suppose, one interprets this on a fairly abstract level, but it can also be applied to physical action. One finds this idea in Zen, which in Japan had a profound influence on the arts of archery and swordsmanship. It was specially prominent in Taoism, which provides, in Chuang Tzu's celebrated story of King Hui's butcher, perhaps the best-known description of how enlightenment leads to skill in action.

The butcher has cut up bullocks for nineteen years without once having had to sharpen his chopper. He explains that this is because he takes advantage of the natural interstices, but he insists that his artistry is not mere skill; it is due to his attunement to the inner nature of existence, the Tao. The king fully understands the significance of this, and remarks that "from the words of Ting the Cook we may learn how to nourish our life".[6]

It may seem strange to link a commonplace or even distasteful activity such as chopping up a bullock with the sublime Tao, but the attitude of mind is typical of Taoism, and turns up in many other Taoists stories in connection with musicians, cicada catchers, boatmen, swimmers, sword-makers, bellstand carvers, arrow-makers, and wheelwrights.* So far as TM is concerned it does seem possible that improved fine tuning of the brain mechanisms which control action would lead to the spontaneous improvement of various skills. A potter who practises TM has told me about an experience which seems to support this idea.

"Throwing" in pottery—the shaping of objects on the wheel —requires as a first step that the mass of clay be accurately centred. This is not as easy as it might seem, for the pressure which is applied must be nicely judged—not too little, not too much. It demands, in fact, a finely adjusted motor system.

The potter of whom I write had at one time tried to throw, but finding centring unexpectedly difficult had gone on to other pottery techniques which do not require the use of a wheel. About two years later she tried throwing again, and found to her surprise that she now had no difficulty in centring the mass of clay.

This suggests to me that her motor skill had improved spontaneously in the intervening period as a result of attaining finer tuning through TM. One swallow does not make a summer, of course, and I would not want to claim much on the basis of a single case; but this story does suggest to me that it might be worth testing people on various tasks requiring co-ordination of hand and eye before starting TM and at various intervals later, to see whether any spontaneous improvement occurs.

Indirect Evidence

The most valuable kind of indirect evidence to support my hypothesis about TM would be findings which showed that the brain really is built up on fine-tuning principles. This is equivalent to asking for a comprehensive understanding of the way the brain works. I need hardly say that we are a very long way from that. The books mentioned in the Bibliography will give an overview of the present state of knowledge about

* It is tempting to see an echo of this attitude in the enthusiasm of modern Chinese Communists for invoking the thoughts of Chairman Mao in the most unlikely-seeming contexts.

the brain; my own feeling is that the picture which emerges is at least compatible with the fine-tuning theory, and indeed that theory was suggested to me by reading these books, especially Pribram's *Languages of the Brain*.

There is one aspect of modern thinking about the brain which perhaps deserves special mention here. In recent years it has become apparent that the brain is capable of change. This is important, because it is a fundamental claim of SCI that TM produces actual, theoretically measurable, alterations in brain structure and function, and that these are the physical basis of the various higher states of consciousness.

Now, until fairly recently this might have seemed a rash claim. The picture of the central nervous system that emerged from textbooks was of a structure that is more or less fixed by the time of birth or soon afterwards. In particular, its capacity for regeneration and repair was thought to be very small. If nerve cells are destroyed they do not regenerate (unlike, say, the cells of the skin or liver), and indeed it is probable that many nerve cells in the brain die each day, although fortunately there is such a large functional surplus that the loss does not impair our intellectual power except perhaps in advanced old age. Again, if nerve fibres in the brain or spinal cord are cut they do not regrow; once a communication is broken it is broken for good.

However, these are fairly gross phenomena, and at the subtler levels the position seems to be different. Actually, it is obvious that the nervous system must have some capacity for changing its chemical composition or physical structure (or both), otherwise learning and memory would be impossible. But in recent years exciting evidence of the "plasticity" of the central nervous system has appeared. For example, Dr J. E. Rose and his associates have shown that if subtle damage to the cortex of rabbits is caused by bombardment with heavy particles (deuterons), new nerve sprouts appear in the damaged area and reconstitute the normal appearance surprisingly closely. This is remarkable enough; but Rose goes on to suggest that growth of nerve fibres in the brain occurs not only when there is damage but continuously, as a part of the normal body processes of change. He is careful to point out that at present this can be but a supposition.

It is not my purpose here to suggest that a continuous growth of central axons [nerve fibres] necessarily occurs under physiological conditions. The point to be made is merely that, under the conditions of our experiments, a massive growth of nerve fibres can actually be shown to take place in the cerebral cortex and that the available evidence appears to be *compatible* with the presumption that this growth may in fact be due to a physiological perpetual growth of central neurons.[7]

We should not be misled by the proper scientific caution which Rose uses in expressing himself. His findings are revolutionary, for they show that the nervous system is not, as the classical view would have it, a fixed structure, but one that is subject to at least the possibility of constant growth and change.

Other findings point in the same direction. It has been shown that the brains of rats which are reared in a stimulating environment, with plenty of opportunity for playing and solving problems, have thicker cortices than do the brains of rats reared in the dark. Part of this difference is due to increase in the number of branchings of basal dendrites—nerve fibres which extend horizontally in the cortex. Much of it, however, is due to an increase in the number of "glue" cells, which hold the nerve cells and fibres together. These glue cells (glial cells), unlike the nerve cells, can multiply. They are usually supposed to be there merely as scaffolding, playing no part in the more exalted activities of memory and thinking. The possibility exists, however, that they have been hiding their light under a bushel. Pribram, among others, believes that these cells may turn out to play an important part in the memory mechanism.[8]

If these views turn out to be even partially right, here is at least the foundation for a concept of "stress release". They give a conceptual solidity for Maharishi's account of TM which I find satisfying. Maharishi, as I have said, has always insisted that TM must produce actual changes in the brain, even if present-day science is unable to detect them. We now have good evidence for thinking that such changes are at least possible, and we can begin to speculate about what form those changes might take.

TM and Sleep

Another line of research which seems to me to have a good deal of indirect relevance to TM is sleep research. I think it is worth spending a little while looking at this, because, as I pointed out in Chapter Two, it is a basic postulate of Maharishi's teaching that TM provides deep rest, and in fact there are a number of interesting similarities between TM and sleep.

It is surely remarkable that mammals should spend so much of their time in that strange state we call sleep, and perhaps even more remarkable is our ignorance about why they (and we) do so. Until about 1960 very few scientific studies of sleep had been made, but today a vast amount of research on the subject is appearing in the psychological journals. Nevertheless, the fundamental questions about what sleep is and the functions it serves seem as far from a solution as ever.

The most important tool used by the researchers into sleep is our old friend the EEG. Sleep produces certain typical EEG changes. As the subject becomes drowsy, the EEG becomes irregular and slower, and so-called "sleep spindles" appear— that is, bursts of activity at about fourteen cycles per second. As sleep becomes deeper the background rhythm becomes slower and slower, eventually reaching one to four cycles per second, although the spindles may continue to appear super-imposed on the basic rhythm.

The depth of sleep does not remain constant throughout the night; instead it fluctuates about every 90 minutes, so that in a whole night's sleep there is a cyclical variation from deep to shallow sleep and back again, though with an over-all trend towards shallower sleep as the night wears on.

For many years this description was thought to be fairly complete. More recently, however, it has been shown that at the crest of each wave the sleeper enters a quite different phase of sleep which is not merely "lighter" but has special characteristics which differentiate it both from deep sleep and from waking, although it is closer to waking than to deep sleep. In this state the EEG is similar to that seen in drowsiness, but there is often some slow alpha activity and sometimes other types of waves occur as well.

Other physiological changes are associated with this phase of sleep. The eyes move about rapidly, as if they were scanning a scene. Blood pressure, heart rate, and breathing become irregular. Muscular jerks may occur, although the anti-gravity muscles, especially those of the neck, relax. At this time the cortex is apparently very excitable.

It was soon discovered that if people were awakened during this "rapid eye movement" phase, they almost always said that they had been dreaming, whereas if they were awakened at other times they either reported no dreams at all or said that they had been thinking, but not with the rich visual imagery which usually characterizes dreaming.

This discovery settles the old argument about whether everyone dreams, and, if so, for how long. It now seems pretty certain that we all dream for about a quarter of the night. During a typical night's sleep, we pass from drowsiness into a phase of deep, dreamless sleep lasting about 90 minutes. We then emerge from this and dream for some minutes before reverting to ordinary sleep. Dreaming sleep recurs roughly every hour and a half for the rest of the night, and lasts longer on each occasion; the final episode usually lasts about half an hour.

A great many names have been given to the two kinds of sleep. Thus, the phase in which dreaming occurs has been called "rapid eye movement" (REM) sleep, and also "para-doxical sleep", because of the investigators' surprise at its resemblance to the waking state. The other phase has been called non-REM sleep and also "deep sleep", but some people have objected to the second term on the grounds that the relative depths of the two kinds of sleep depend on the criteria one chooses to measure them by. Here I shall use the common-sense terms "dreaming sleep" and "deep sleep", since whatever questions they may beg they are at least easy to keep in one's mind.

So much for a very brief outline of the physiology of sleep. But what is sleep *for*?

To the layman this is likely to seem a foolish question; we sleep to restore our bodies and minds when they are fatigued. The scientist, however, tends to be less at his ease with questions about purpose, and indeed some researchers refuse to speculate about the purpose of sleep at all. Not all scientists have been so ultra-cautious, however, and a useful summary of theories on the subject can be found in a recent book, *The Functions of Sleep*, by Dr Ernest L. Hartmann.

Most theories of sleep suggest that it allows for the occurrence of some form of repair. But what is being repaired? And do the two phases of sleep serve the same function or different ones. (Some researchers have gone so far as to deny that the dreaming phase is really part of sleep at all, and have preferred to look on it as a third physiological state, additional to waking and sleep.) We do not know the answers to these questions, but some clues exist.

One useful line of approach is to look at sleep in other animals. Sleep is found in all the higher vertebrates—reptiles, birds, and mammals; whether amphibians and fish sleep is doubtful. The lower vertebrates, however, show principally deep sleep. Dreaming sleep is mainly a mammalian acquisition, although it does occur for brief periods in birds.[9]

These facts suggest that sleep, and especially dreaming sleep, is somehow associated with the possession of an elaborate brain. It is tempting to speculate that the more advanced your brain structure, the more you need to dream. Support for this idea comes from a report that the spiny ant-eater, a very primitive mammal, does not show dreaming sleep; but, in general, there are no clear-cut differences in sleep or dreaming sleep requirements among the various species of mammals. Contrary to what one might expect, the higher mammals, such as monkeys and apes, do not differ much as regards their sleeping patterns from lower forms.[10]

An alternative approach is to look at the way sleep develops in the individual. We find that the newborn child spends some sixteen to eighteen hours of each day asleep, and at least half of this time is spent in the dreaming phase. It seems probable that, before birth, the foetus spends even more time in the "dreaming" phase.[11] (Obviously this is a case in which the terminology becomes a little difficult; it is fascinating, but unprofitable, to speculate about our pre-natal dreams.) These facts suggest that dreaming is specially associated with growth and development.

The need of adults for dreaming sleep has been studied in experiments on volunteers, who were selectively deprived of this form of sleep for various periods up to sixteen successive nights by Dr W. C. Dement. Experiments of this kind have shown that there is apparently a "need to dream"; at any rate, if people are deprived of dreaming they build up a "dreaming debt" and dream for long periods (as shown by the EEG) when allowed to do so. Another interesting finding in Dement's experiments was that some subjects developed (fortunately temporary) personality disturbances. One, for instance, underwent a Jekyll-and-Hyde personality change; from being somewhat taciturn and inhibited, he became garrulous and impulsive, and showed a quite uncharacteristic taste for rowdy night clubs, in which he deliberately created a disturbance to get himself thrown out. Another became very suspicious of everyone about him, and Dement stopped the experiment for fear a full-blown psychosis might develop.[12]

Now, what, you may ask, has all this to do with TM? The answer is that I believe both sleep and TM have a common origin in the evolutionary process. Both are forms of rest; both are natural; and both, I want to suggest, serve broadly similar purposes. The resemblance is particularly close in the case of TM and dreaming sleep.

In his interesting book on sleep, to which I have already referred, Dr Hartmann suggests that the common-sense view of sleep as serving to "knit up the ravelled sleeve of care" by restoring body and mind is basically correct. More specifically, he thinks that deep sleep is needed to restore the body after physical tiredness, and it probably also serves to prepare for the subsequent phase of dreaming sleep.

Dreaming sleep is more complex than deep sleep, Hartmann believes. From a comparative study of the psychological characteristics of people who sleep for varying periods, he concludes that dreaming sleep serves to repair the results of stress. This phase of sleep is specially required, he believes, by "persons who have, disrupted their usual ways of doing things, who have, often stressfully, reprogrammed themselves during their waking hours".[13]

Hartmann sees dreaming sleep as being specially concerned with recovery from mental tiredness. I should like to quote his description of this form of tiredness, because of its relevance to the concept of the brain which I am using in this book.

The body can be seen as an extremely delicate set of balances and homeostatic adjustments, each delicately tuned and each generally in a state of stable equilibrium; this is especially true of the central nervous system. Tiredness affects these balanced mechanisms so that there is a less delicate balance or tuning. In extreme tiredness there is less of the usual delicate "buffering": a small external input can produce a large perturbation which is not immediately and smoothly damped out as it would normally be.[14]

It is tempting to speculate on the nature of these perturbations. Hartmann himself believes that they are probably structural, and are related to the mechanism of memory formation. This idea, of course, brings his concept of stress very close to the one I have suggested in relation to TM.

In general, there seem to be two main theories about the neurological basis of fatigue and stress. One says that fatigue is produced by a decrease in the activity of nerve cells, either throughout the brain or selectively, in certain areas. One way in which this might occur would be if activity entailed the production of a chemical which accumulated and interfered with nervous activity; the function of rest would then be to dissipate the chemical. Conversely, fatigue could occur through the depletion of a chemical, and rest might then be required to reconstitute it.

The alternative theory proposes that fatigue is due, not to under-activity, but to over-activity. If stimulation of the brain continued too intensely or too long, the sensitivity of brain cells might increase to such an extent that they began to become active spontaneously. In that case the amount of "noise" within the brain—that is, the amount of unproductive activity, not related to the carrying of information—would increase. This would interfere with the highest-grade activities selectively, because these demand the greatest number of channels to carry the large amount of information which they make use of. According to A. T. Welford:

Such rises in sensitivity could result from the neural activity produced by immediately present stresses or sometimes perhaps from the facilitative after-effects, often lasting several minutes, of prolonged stimulation of nerve cells. The cells would be made hypersensitive; though in moderate degrees this would raise the sensitivity of the system, in more severe degrees it would make cells liable to be fired by any random activity in the brain and especially by after-discharges from previous activity. Discussions in this area have tended to stress general arousal or activation, but the same principle could clearly apply to restricted brain mechanisms.[15]

As Welford goes on to point out, the two theories of fatigue are not mutually exclusive; indeed, they may well both be true, some fatigue being due to over-activity and some to under-activity. On the basis of one's own experience, it certainly seems likely that mental fatigue—the kind of fatigue which occurs after an exciting day, or when one is worried, and which may actually prevent one from getting to sleep—is due to over-activity.

Dreaming sleep seems to remove this form of tiredness. Indeed, it may do more. When one has a problem, one is often advised to "sleep on it". This advice often proves sound; next morning, the problem seems to have shrunk, and to be much less intimidating; sometimes, even, the solution presents itself to one on awakening. On Hartmann's theory, the explanation for this would be that, during dreaming sleep, the highest brain centres are "shunted out" and reorganized, so that new connections can be made.

I believe that susceptibility to stress, and therefore need for rest, is correlated with the degree of evolution of the nervous system. At the human level at least three kinds of stress occur, and therefore three kinds of rest have evolved.

Phylogenetically, the oldest form of rest is deep sleep, which appears to be principally concerned with physical restoration of the body. At the next level there emerges dreaming sleep, which, I have suggested, allows for structural repair of the nervous system at a more subtle level—that is, at the level where (presumably) memories are recorded. Finally, at the third level we find TM, which is concerned with repairing the effects of those forms of stress which affect human beings almost exclusively.

Whenever the brain fails to resolve a discrepancy between two sets of information, or between information and memory, the record of that failure is stored within the brain, possibly holographically. This record will serve as an irritative focus, raising the local and general noise level against which incoming signals have to compete. Moreover, although it does not necessarily continue to affect thinking, and the original precipitating event is "forgotten", it can be re-activated later whenever the disposition of the brain—the configuration of the images it contains—triggers the sensitive area.

A stress, in other words, is like an old wound, often forgotten but making itself felt whenever the weather turns wet.

TM appears to be the way which the brain has evolved for neutralizing these areas of disturbance. It does not replace deep sleep or dreaming; rather, it is complementary, because it deals with different forms of stress. Nevertheless, there is probably some overlap. Hartmann mentions[16] that he has been told by people practising TM that their sleep requirements gradually fell by one or two hours after they began to meditate, and I agree that this is a common—though by no means universal—effect of TM. I infer that, for many non-meditators, sleep is attempting to resolve stresses for which it is not suited and which can be fully resolved only by TM; this is why the need for sleep falls off when TM is started.

An apparent TM effect which I have noticed in my own case and had reported to me by many other meditators is a change in the *quality* of dreaming. There seems to be a tendency for dreams to become more and more transparently related to the events of the preceding day; the elaborate Freudian "disguises" seem gradually to disappear. I mention this in passing, as a matter of interest; I am not sure what the explanation is, though it is tempting to speculate that the depth of "unconscious mind" is decreasing, allowing material to enter consciousness more directly.

I have dwelt on the resemblances and relationships between TM and sleep because they seem to me important both for the light they shed on TM and for their research implications. I think that TM probably produces a number of changes in the physiology of sleep, and EEG studies of sleep in meditators might well give interesting results. Perhaps, for instance, the duration of dreaming sleep alters in meditators, or the EEG pattern in either or both phases of sleep may be different from what is found in non-meditators. (Banquet claims that he has, in fact, found some differences of this kind.)

Biofeedback

To conclude this chapter, I want to say a few words about

the currently fashionable cult of biofeedback. In the last few years it has been found that, if people are given information about what their body is doing, they can often influence it in surprising ways. For example, many people have successfully controlled their own blood pressure, relieved migraines, and produced alpha activity on the EEG. It is the last feat which is supposedly relevant to meditation. The argument is that meditation is associated with alpha activity; biofeedback produces alpha; therefore biofeedback and meditation produce the same psychophysical effects. Some people see biofeedback as an electronic gateway to mystical experience, and biofeedback seems likely to undergo an apotheosis similar to that which overtook LSD a few years ago.

The flaw in the argument I have outlined above is fairly evident. Alpha activity is merely one aspect of the state brought about by TM; it is the one which the rather crude apparatus known as the EEG has chanced to reveal. There may well be, and probably are, all sorts of other effects on the brain and other parts of the body which have nothing to do with alpha rhythm. Merely producing this rhythm will not, therefore, have the same effects as TM, and indeed people who have tried both report that subjectively the two states are quite different.

The essential point to grasp is that alpha activity—and, indeed, all the other physiological effects of TM—are by-products of the meditation process, not its goal. Deliberately inducing various EEG rhythms may or may not be valuable, but it is very unlikely to bring about all the mental and physical benefits of TM. At best, the states induced by biofeedback bear much the same relation to TM as drug-induced sleep does to natural sleep.

X

Creativity

I HAVE NOW said as much as I intend to about the physiological aspects of TM. One of Maharishi's most important and far-reaching claims still remains to be considered, however; I mean his claim that TM enhances creativity. People who practise TM and who are engaged in some form of intellectual or artistic activity usually do say that their work has improved since starting to meditate, but of course it is open to the sceptic to dismiss this as self-suggestion. To demonstrate that it is not would be an enormous undertaking, requiring the collection and assessment not only of subjective reports from meditators but also of objective studies by critics and psychologists; it would also require what is still lacking today—an adequate definition of creativity and a satisfactory way of measuring it. The task requires tackling, but this is not the place for it.

My approach will be different. I want to look at the psychological experience of the creative process itself to see whether it resembles the experience of TM. I believe that important resemblances do in fact exist, and these resemblances seem to me to provide at least a *prima facie* case for supposing that TM really does enhance creativity. In brief, I shall suggest that the creative process can best be understood in terms of the cycle of differentiation, and that this is the reason why TM and creativity are so closely linked.

Let me start by setting out what I take to be the essentials of the creative experience. Generalizations about anything as individual as creativity are bound to be hazardous; nevertheless, one can isolate an underlying pattern or ground rhythm from the descriptions which artists, scientists, and others have given of their own creative activity.

Creation falls into a number of stages:

1. *Identification of the Problem.* A more or less clear awareness of a difficulty or need arises in the mind, and sets in train the search for a solution.

2. *Pondering and Reflection.* Over a period which may be

anything from minutes to almost a lifetime, attempts are made to collect information relevant to the problem and to arrange it into a satisfying pattern. Eventually this phase passes, more or less suddenly, into the next.

3. *Resolution*. This is typically brief, lasting a few minutes or even less. It is this phase which is often called "inspiration". A new pattern is suddenly generated to accommodate the material which has been accumulated in the preceding phase.

4. *Testing*. This requires that the insight gained in the third phase be expressed in a practical or communicable form and applied, in some sense, to the real world. At this stage the insight may be wholly accepted or wholly rejected, or it may be accepted partially. In that case, it is returned for further processing, in which case the same sequence of events will recur, with the insight gained in stage three forming part of the material for a new stage one.

Now, it should be evident that what I have just outlined is simply the cycle of differentiation under another name. Stages one and two correspond to increasing degrees of imbalance; stage three is gaining of balance; and stage four is the new sensitivity which results from the reorganization which occurred as stage three was reached.

If this is so, it follows that stages one and two ought to be accompanied by feelings of unrest or even unhappiness, while stage three ought to produce happiness. And accounts of the creative experience show that this is in fact the case. This has been brought out with special clarity by a writer who is not a professional psychologist—Marghanita Laski. In her remarkable study *Ecstasy* she made a detailed examination of material derived both from published literary and religious texts and also from a questionnaire answered by some 60-odd of her friends and acquaintances. On this basis she developed a view of creativity as occurring in five stages, namely, (1) the asking of the question, (2) the collection of material, (3) the "fusing" of the material, (4) the translation of the "fused" material into communicable form, and (5) the testing of the answer.[1]

At the moment of fusing, she believes, there may occur an "ecstatic" experience, which is actually a form of mystical experience. Miss Laski's main purpose, in fact, seems to have been to develop an explanation of mystical experience which should be non-religious and yet should not denigrate it, since

Miss Laski, though a rationalist, believes that ecstatic experience is "normal" and indeed supremely valuable. These experiences, she believes, "are manifestations (probably exaggerated manifestations) of the processes facilitating improved mental organization".[2] Her development of these ideas is subtle and ingenious, but I do not want to discuss it here (I have done so in more detail in *Seven States of Consciousness*); my purpose is only to draw attention to her scheme of creativity and to emphasize the part played in it by the moment of fusion.

Schemes of this general kind have been proposed by a number of other writers. G. Wallas, for example, in *The Art of Thought*, has four stages—Preparation, Incubation, Illumination ("the appearance of the 'happy idea' together with the psychological events which immediately preceded and accompanied that appearance"), and Verification.[3] F. L. Lucas, likewise, suggests a method of writing which falls roughly into four stages; at the core of his scheme is an alternation between "surface" and "deep" thought. His stages are as follows:

1. (a) Meditation and documentation.
   (b) Incubation.
2. Periods of alternate thought, quick writing, and partial revision, till the first draft is complete.
3. Revision; further documentation, correction, curtailment, and amplification. This can be repeated indefinitely, subject to the danger of the book's growing unwieldly, overloaded, or stale.[4]

Here again we see the cycle of differentiation at work.

Two important points emerge from all this, and I want to spend a little time looking at each of them in turn. The first is the connection between creativity and happiness, and the second is the nature of creative thought.

Creativity and Happiness

I have already mentioned Miss Laski's theory—which I believe to be broadly correct—that ecstasy is linked with the attainment of mental organization and so with creativity. In the light of the concept of the cycle of differentiation, I

would go even further and suggest that one of the principle
springs of activity in the higher mammals, including ourselves,
is the *quest for balance* (in physiological terms) or the *quest for
pattern* (in psychological terms). If we are talking about the
brain, I say that the various homeostats in the core and
elsewhere are constantly seeking to gain stability; if we are
talking about the mind, I say that its contents are constantly
trying to arrange themselves into the most stable configuration.

The human mind is so constructed that it is always seeking
to make sense of its surroundings, so much so that it will make
a pattern even when no real pattern exists. Everyone must have
lain in bed at some time and made up faces from marks on the
wall. In much the same way, if one listens for some time to a
conversation in a totally unknown language, such as Chinese,
one will suddenly seem to hear, quite distinctly, a word or
phrase in English. The brain is trying to make bricks without
straw, finding non-existent patterns because any pattern is
better than none.

Delight in solving problems is far from being an exclusively
human characteristic. Surprising though it may seem, there is
no doubt that the higher mammals, at any rate, actually enjoy
solving problems. An interesting illustration of this comes from
some experiments carried out a few years ago in Wisconsin.
Four monkeys were given mechanical problems to solve and
were rewarded for getting them right, while another four
monkeys were given the same puzzles but were not rewarded.
The monkeys who were rewarded solved all the puzzles, while
only one of the unbribed monkeys did so; this one simian
Daedalus, however, was as quick at the work as those who had
an ulterior motive. But what was specially remarkable about
the experiment was that all the monkeys who were not rewarded
continued to play with the puzzles, whereas those who had
received a reward lost interest in the puzzles as soon as they
had solved them. Indeed, one of the reasons why the disin-
terested monkeys mostly failed to reach the correct solution
was that they became so wrapped up in investigating the
properties of their new toys.[5]

This observation does not stand alone; other studies of
monkeys, chimpanzees, and orang-utans have yielded similar
results. It may seem excessively anthropomorphic to say so,
but I think we must regard the monkeys who played with the

puzzles as primitive scientists, for science is essentially problem solving. (Indeed, we must call the unrewarded monkeys pure scientists, since they were motivated wholly by the desire for understanding.)

The apes have preceded us not only as scientists but also as artists. As is by now well known, chimpanzees apparently enjoy painting pictures when given the equipment to do so, and Jane Goodall has described how wild chimpanzees perform an ecstatic rain dance during thunderstorms; Terpsichore, it seems, has a long ancestry, and was born in Africa.[6] What is the motive power behind art? I believe it is the same as lies behind science—the quest for a pattern. The difference between art and science is more one of materials than of principle.

An artist tries to create a pattern. This is specially obvious in the case of painting, but the same is true of the other arts. The composer often speaks of "balancing" a composition, the poet creates interwoven patterns of meaning, sound, and rhythm, and so on. But the creating of patterns and the solving of problems are not very far apart. In a recent television interview, the sculptor Henry Moore said that he was trying to make forms *which would be impossible to draw*. What else could such forms be except puzzles?

Even games and sports can be seen in terms of pattern-making and problem-solving. The rules are usually devised so as to make the difficulties as great as possible without becoming insuperable. Golf courses, for example, are deliberately designed to provide traps for the less skilful; anglers use light tackle to "give the fish a chance"; serious hunters despise those who shoot sitting birds with shotguns, and so on. And in sport, as in art and science, the roots seem to go far back in evolution. Animals *enjoy* exercising their hunting skills. A pet cat, for example, though well fed, does not spend its entire life curled up in front of the fire; it goes out in the gardens and fields to catch birds and mice, which it frequently brings back in triumph to the feet of its appalled owner. The skills required to catch a mouse, or shoot a pheasant, or knock a ball into a little cup in the ground provide satisfaction when they are exercised. In games and sports, people develop and use primitive skills which would have been useful to a hunter—running, swimming, riding, throwing, and co-ordination of hand and eye generally. All forms of sport could be looked on as *physical problems* which it is the task of the participants to solve, and which provide satisfaction in the solving.

From this it will be evident that I am linking creativity with play. Play is actually a most interesting phenomenon. Far from being something trivial which one does when more serious matters are not occupying one to better purpose, play seems to be very important in the development of the mammalian brain. It is largely confined to the higher mammals, and even among these it is mainly the young which play. The exceptions to this rule are principally human beings and their pets, and in both cases there is an element of paedomorphosis—that is, human beings and also the domestic cat and dog retain a number of physical features, such as the shapes of their skulls, which are characteristic of the young of their wild relatives (apes, tigers, wolves). Play, likewise, is a juvenile characteristic which persists into adult life.

This is probably significant, because in evolution new species seem to arise, not from a fully developed and mature strain, but from a more primitive and undifferentiated forebear. Juvenile physical features, that is, seem to be associated with the ability to change and evolve; and perhaps the same is true of juvenile mental features too.

At all events, in both human beings and other mammals, play seems to serve a necessary function in fostering the development of the nervous system. It is, in fact, a very important part of learning and maturation; the proverb about all work and no play has a great deal of profundity. Without play, the higher forms of mental life are probably impossible.

Indeed, if we jump for a moment to the metaphysical level, we find that Indian philosophy applies the word *lila* (play) to the principle of cosmic evolution. Creation itself is seen as a form of divine play; hence the frequent representations in Indian iconography of Siva dancing. There seems to be a deep psychological connection between play and creativity, and I am sure that we have here a most important clue to understanding the common spring that gives rise to science, art, and even religion.

The human brain—and therefore the human mind—seems to be built in such a way that it always tends to organize all the information it contains into a comprehensive whole. The aesthetic appeal of a great work of art, or of a scientific theory, is that it represents a new synthesis. And when we experience the work or comprehend the theory, we recreate the creative act within ourselves, at least to some extent, and this provides satisfaction, sometimes even ecstasy. (In Miss Laski's study, art was a frequent "trigger" for ecstasy.)

The reason we call one work of art "greater" than another is probably connected with the comprehensiveness of the pattern to which it gives rise in the mind of its audience. When we read *War and Peace*, or contemplate the Sistine Chapel, or listen to the *St Matthew Passion*, we experience a sense of wholeness. For the moment, at least, many contraries have been resolved, and the mind is at peace. The depth of happiness which ensues seems to depend on the amount of material which has been unified. *Emma* is a near-perfect novel, but it is not on the same scale as *War and Peace* and does not—for most people—produce as great a sense of resolution, even though it may be, in its own way, more perfect. A detective story may be, within its set limits, wholly satisfying, but the limits are very narrow and the sense of resolution comparatively trivial.

The real reason why disputes about the qualities of different works of art can never be resolved comes down, I think, to this: that the furniture of people's minds differs, and therefore what is a supreme resolution for one person may not be so for another. A work of art has no meaning by itself, any more than gold has value to a man on a desert island; it has meaning and value only in a context.

All this may seem obvious enough, but the point I want to emphasize is that the appeal of art and science can be understood as an expression of the cycle of differentiation. Art and science should be understood in an evolutionary context, a point which has been well brought out by the critic I. A. Richards. "We should not forget that *finer organization* [my italics] is the most successful way of relieving strain, a fact of relevance in the theory of evolution. The new response will be more advantageous than the old, more successful in satisfying varied appetencies."[7]

From my argument it follows that what we call mystical experience *is the creative experience in its purest form*. In mystical experience—which is the root of religion—*all* tensions, *all* contradictions, are temporarily resolved, and perfect harmony and balance are attained. Typically it is mystical experience which gives rise to "totality explanations", which seek to provide answers to all possible questions.

In a broadcast discussion in 1948, Bertrand Russell and Father F. C. Copleston, a Jesuit, argued this point. Father Copleston said that the problem was "the question of the existence of the whole of this sorry scheme of things, of the whole universe . . . An adequate explanation must ultimately be a total explanation, to which nothing further could be added." To this, Russell replied: "Then I can only say that you are looking for something which can't be got, and which one ought not to expect to get."[8]

Whether one *ought* to expect it or not, it seems that the reason one frequently *does* expect it is that one's brain is so constructed that one should. Totality explanations arise because of the organizing capacity of the mind and the tendency of the brain to seek for equilibrium.*

Whether or not they have validity is another question, to which I shall return in a later chapter, when I consider the connection between the working of our brains and "cosmic law".

The Nature of Creative Thought

I now want to look at what happens in the mind at the moment of fusion, or inspiration, when the problem is resolved, the pattern completed, and creation actually occurs. What is creative thought like? And how does it differ, if at all, from ordinary thought?

Thought is a notoriously difficult thing to define or describe. If asked, most people would probably say that they think in a confused jumble of words and pictures, out of which speech and actions emerge in an unexpectedly coherent and organized manner. But even if this is true of ordinary mortals, surely it cannot be the case with those superior beings we call geniuses, especially mathematical and scientific geniuses? *They* at least, you might suppose, conduct their internal deliberations in "pure thought" or in symbolic terms. You would, however, be

* It is interesting that Russell himself originally took up philo-sophy in the hope of getting a totality explanation. On this, see *Portraits from Memory*, p. 16.

wrong. When they are being creative, at any rate, they seem almost invariably to think in *images*. Here, for example, is Albert Einstein.

> The words of the language, as they are written or spoken, do not seem to play any rôle in my mechanism of thought. The physical entities which seem to serve as elements in thought are certain signs and more or less clear images which can be "voluntarily" reproduced and combined ... The above-mentioned elements are, in any case, of visual and some of muscular type. Conventional words of other signs have to be sought for laboriously only in a secondary stage, when the mentioned associative play is sufficiently established and can be reproduced at will.[10]

This passage is quoted by Koestler from J. Hadamard's book *The Psychology of Invention in the Mathematical Field*. Hadamard, himself a mathematician, found that almost all the mathematicians he interrogated avoided the mental use of words and other symbols, including algebraic ones, preferring to think in images which were usually visual but might, as in Einstein's case, be auditory or even kinaesthetic.

As Koestler rightly points out, this dependence of creative thought on vague imagery to the exclusion of language is in sharp contradiction to the widely accepted notion that thought is synonymous with interior *speech*, and that the evolution of human intellectual activity was bound up with the evolution of language. Indeed, the early behaviourists went so far as to assert that thinking is nothing more than subliminal whispering to oneself. But the descriptions I have quoted—and they could easily be augmented from many sources—make it quite clear that creative thinking, at any rate, is almost always conducted not in words but in images.

Although there are some variations in details, almost every writer on creativity I have read has recognized the existence of two levels of thinking: a "surface" level, which is under "conscious" control, and a "deep" level which is the source of new ideas but which cannot be deliberately manipulated.*

* You may wonder why I do not call this deep level the unconscious and have done with it. Is that not, after all, what I mean? My answer is that I do not think the term "unconscious" is a very

Thinking at deep levels differs from surface thinking in certain important ways. First, as I have said, it is "imagey" rather than verbal. Second, the images tend to combine with one another in patterns, and this is the clue to the creative process, for it is in this way that new ideas come to birth. (There are interesting relationships between these two forms of thinking and the categories of logical and correlative thinking which I mentioned in Chapter Five.) This tendency to form combinations has been called "bisociation" by Koestler, who sees it as a common denominator in jokes, science, and art. The same idea seems to underlie Edward De Bono's distinction between "vertical" and "lateral" thinking.[11] Lateral thinking, with its readiness to consider new possibilities and combinations of ideas, without regard for illogicalities and *non sequiturs*, is at the heart of all original thinking.

As an example (mine, not De Bono's), consider the story of the candidate at a postgraduate examination in medicine, who told the examiner that he had heard a particular murmur. The examiner disagreed. The "vertical thinking" answer would have been to accept the examiner's verdict, and perhaps fail the examination. The candidate, however, was more resourceful. "Ah," he said, "the trouble is that your stethoscope is not sensitive enough. Please try mine." And so taken aback was the examiner that he "heard" the murmur, and the candidate passed.

The essence of all new ideas is the formation of unexpected patterns. The mathematician Henri Poincaré compared the mind to a room containing the elements of ideas, which he pictured as something like hooked atoms. During complete mental inactivity, they lie dormant on the wall. During creative thinking, on the other hand, they become detached and fly about, joining up at random into new patterns. The choice of which atoms shall be put into activity in this way depends on the preliminary "surface" thinking.

But what determines which of the many combinations so formed shall emerge into the light of day? According to Poin-

---

happy one. The deep levels are not unconscious but only unfamiliar. The creative person is the one for whom they are conscious and accessible, and the task of the creator is to mediate between these levels and the surface.

caré, the determining factors are beauty and elegance. "The useful combinations are precisely the most beautiful, I mean those best able to charm this special sensibility that all mathematicians know, but of which the profane are so ignorant as often to be tempted to smile at it."[12]

This seems to me most important, for here we find once more common ground between science and art. Poincaré is not alone among scientists and mathematicians in feeling like this; Einstein and Dirac, to name but two, have expressed similar ideas. It appears that for many mathematicians and scientists if not for all, the "beauty" of an idea is the surest guide to its rightness. What seems to have happened in the case of many great discoveries in science is that the solution is first glimpsed in its entirety, and the intervening step—the logical proof—comes later. This is very much like what happens in art; thus, a novelist often starts out with a general feeling about where he is going and what his book will be about, but few novelists have a detailed plan at the outset and even fewer stick to any plan they may have.

In neurological terms, the sense of beauty and elegance is due, I believe, to the attainment of balance within the brain. A solution to a problem of any kind, scientific or artistic, is felt to be satisfying when it restores the brain to balance.

Beauty is thus our guide to truth; but it is important to realize that she may be a deceiver. Poincaré discusses this problem.

> I have spoken of the feeling of absolute certitude accompanying the inspiration; in the cases cited this feeling was no deceiver, nor is it usually. But do not think that this is a rule without exception; often this feeling deceives us without being any the less vivid, and we find it out when we seek to put on foot the demonstration.[13]

Most scientists and artists who have discussed the question seem to agree that there is no subjective difference between the valid inspiration and the invalid. The idea which turns out to be wrong arrives with just as strong a sense of conviction as does the idea which turns out to be triumphantly right, and there seems to be no way of distinguishing between the two except by trying them out. It is not easy to see why this should be so, but tentatively I would offer the following explanation.

Whenever a new pattern is formed in the brain—whenever two sets of images are fused into a third—balance is restored and we experience satisfaction. But this is a purely internal affair, and there is no guarantee that the newly formed image will bear any relation to the outer world. This is why previous "surface" work is so important; someone who has accumulated a great deal of knowledge about a subject is obviously far more likely to attain a fruitful insight than someone who knows little about it. Even the greatest human mind is not omniscient, however, and therefore may from time to time achieve a faulty synthesis—that is, a synthesis which works in that it resolves tensions and so produces an immediate sense of satisfaction and conviction, but which does not relate properly to the outer world. No doubt the greater the genius of the individual, the less likely is it that such false inspirations will occur, but they cannot be excluded even in the case of the greatest. Even Homer may nod.

Separating the wheat from the chaff requires the use of "logical", "surface", "vertical" thinking, and this is the final phase of the creativity cycle. It is as necessary in its place as the others. If you remain wholly on the surface you are a computer, but if you never surface at all you are a solipsistic madman. The secret of creativity is to move between *both* levels, and to bring the insights gained in the depths out into the world where they can be useful.

Creativity and TM

As I have said, creative and intellectual people who practise TM often claim that their work is better than previously. There are, I suggest, two main reasons for this.

First, creativity comes about through the cycle of differentiation. Since TM accelerates the revolution of that cycle, it is natural that TM should enhance creativity.

Second, "subtle thought" resembles creative thought in being (a) "imagey" and (b) associated with the experience of happiness. Creative thinking and subtle thinking are, I believe, identical.

The "imagey" level of thinking is not the deepest; it is intermediate between the surface level of logical thought and the underlying stillness of pure awareness. Pure awareness is the foundation of all the rest, but the special importance of the "imagey" layer is that it is the region where new combinations of ideas occur.

I do not want to give the impression that each time one meditates one surfaces, like a triumphant pearl fisher, with a new insight. Rather, what happens is that, over a fairly long period, the clarity of thinking and the ability to conceive new ideas gradually increase. The attention seems to begin to oscillate between surface and depth, not merely at special times, but constantly, throughout the day, and the quality of thought as a whole is enriched.

Inspiration

The last question I want to consider in this chapter is the intriguing one of where new ideas come from. Throughout the whole discussion, I have been assuming that new ideas are built up out of smaller units; during artistic and scientific creation, two images combine and give rise to a third which is more comprehensive and all-inclusive.

What is implied here is a "growth" theory of the way the mind evolves. At birth, the infant is confronted with what William James called a "buzzing, blooming confusion", out of which the brain gradually assembles coherent images, and these are progressively combined together to give more and more abstract ideas. This way of looking at the matter is accepted almost without question by almost all Western psychologists and philosophers except Plato.

However, this may be a mistake. F. A. Hayek, Professor of Economics at the University of Freiburg, has made the interesting suggestion that the commonly accepted view puts the cart before the horse. Hayek suggests that our minds are really built in accordance with certain abstract principles, and that these are primary (in both a temporal and a logical sense) to the perception of the concrete.

What I contend, in short, is that the mind must be capable of performing abstracting operations in order to be able to perceive particulars, and that this capacity appears long before we can speak of a conscious awareness of particulars.

Subjectively, we live in a concrete world and may have the greatest difficulty in discovering even a few of the abstract relations which enable us to discriminate between different things and to respond to them differentially. But when we want to explain what makes us tick, we must start with the abstract relations governing the order which, as a whole, gives particulars their place.[14]

This idea, if correct, means that psychology and the theory of knowledge usually begin at the wrong end, by treating as given what most needs to be explained. Hayek's way of looking at the mind has obvious resonances with Plato's concept of Forms and also with Noam Chomsky's views on the origins of language. It also, I think—and this is why I have mentioned it—has a good deal in common with Maharishi's teaching about Creative Intelligence and the source of thought.

As I pointed out in Chapter Two, Maharishi pictures thought as *beginning* at the subtlest, most abstract, region of the mind and proceeding thence towards the gross, concrete levels. A subtle thought is less defined, more vague, than a gross one, but also more all-inclusive and powerful—powerful in the sense that it contains many latent possibilities. On this scheme, it is the subtle thoughts which give rise to the gross ones, not vice versa.

If this idea is right, the process of creation, although it seems like a building up of complex ideas from simpler ones, is really more like a rediscovery of fundamental principles.

Consider Einstein's discovery of the formula $E = mc^2$. This is an example of an insight of supreme genius; and in one sense it is true that Einstein must have made his discovery by starting from what was already known and building up to it. But although he may have arrived at the formula that way, it is not at all complex; indeed, it is so simple that it can be understood by a schoolboy in his first year of physics. And yet the meaning which it encloses is so far-reaching and profound that it has altered the whole way in which physicists conceive of the world and has, of course, irrevocably changed the course of history. So should we call the formula simple or complex?

The answer is that it is both. It is like a seed, containing latent within itself an immense amount of information—but only for someone who can make use of it. In many ways a subtle thought is like this. It is simple, and yet much is latent in it, just as an acorn is potentially an oak tree but only in the right circumstances.

Creation in the scientific or artistic sense usually seems like a building up from simpler to more complex, but perhaps that is an illusion. Perhaps it is really just the reverse, and consists in a return to the Source. If so, there may be more to the metaphor of "inspiration" than the modern mind has usually been willing to concede.

XI

The Logical Levels of Thought

NOT LONG AGO a well-known painter wrote a letter to a national newspaper in which he said that, having lived for some twenty years in a conventional manner, he had begun to find his paintings unsatisfactory. Concluding that the reason must be the lack of stress in his life, he took to riotous living and within a year ended in hospital, having crashed his expensive new car while drunk. His domestic life was in ruins but the reward, so he said, was a great improvement in his art. We were given to understand that the sacrifice had been well worth while.

This real-life enactment of the theme of Joyce Cary's novel *The Horse's Mouth* epitomizes a particularly tenacious modern myth: that the artist is necessarily a wild, uncontrolled Bohemian whose mission is to "create" at whatever cost to himself or anyone else. What might be called the Promethean view of the artist is so much part of Western thought-patterns that the view of creativity which I advanced in the last chapter may seem to some people to raise a difficulty. If creativity is so closely bound up with stress, how can a technique like TM, which is supposed to eliminate stress, be said to favour creativity?

This is a complicated and important question. If I am to answer it, I must first disentangle the various threads which have become woven together to give the picture of creativity we have today. One of these derives from the Romantics, with their emphasis on *sturm und drang*. Another element was supplied by Freud, or more precisely by the popular idea of Freud, according to which the artist is a neurotic who expresses his neuroticism in art and so is enabled as it were to capitalize upon his psychological disability. According to one authority, Richard Wollheim, Freud did not actually hold these views, and the popular idea of what he taught is mistaken.[1] However this may be, popular ideas about what thinkers taught are often more influential than what those thinkers really taught, and the notions that "geniuses are mad" (this pre-dates Freud, of course) and that art is fuelled by neuroticism are deeply entrenched in many people's minds.

No doubt one reason for this is that these ideas provide comfort to people who are suffering. If you are tortured by obsessions or anxiety, it is no doubt some consolation to believe that these disorders may one day provide the compost which will nurture the flower of a great novel; and even if they do not, at least the suffering is a link with greatness, however indirect.

Probably yet another strand is provided by certain Christian teachings on the value of suffering. Although it can be strongly argued that the concept of suffering is not as central to Christianity as some of its apologists would have us believe, nevertheless in practice most Christians—and many agnostics and atheists too—have been brought up in the belief that suffering ennobles and purifies. If this idea be accepted, it is natural to conclude that suffering must play a part in the creative process.

And if theory were not enough, we have the testimony of artists themselves, many of whom have spoken of the "throes of composition" and the "agony of creation". Even if we allow for literary convention, and for an understandable desire on the part of some writers to conceal the fact that they actually enjoy what they get paid for doing, it does seem likely that, for some artists if not for all, creation and stress are in some way linked.

Acceptance of this general view of creativity prompts remarks which one often hears, such as "I need my tensions if I am to work". Indeed, if one believes in the theory of a link between suffering and art, and if one also accepts the modern valuation (over-valuation?) of art, one is naturally brought to the conclusion that there is something almost immoral in ridding oneself of tensions.

These questions are by no means academic, for although most of us may not be artists, we all have to encounter situations of stress—interviews, examinations, public appearances of all kinds—and a great many people insist that, unless they are wound up to a high pitch of anxiety before these occasions, they do not give of their best. To reduce anxiety, as it is claimed TM does, might therefore seem undesirable. So is it true that a degree of stress is needed to call forth our best responses?

In recent years a good deal of research has gone on into this matter, and has led to the concept of "arousal". At present it is held that the reticular activating system in the brain core stimulates or arouses the cortex by sending impulses to it; if the arousal level falls too low one goes to sleep, while if it rises too high one becomes over-excited. In times of stress a high level of arousal is thought to be an advantage because it activates the brain to reach its best working level.

If this idea is correct—and it seems likely that it is, at least in outline—probably the people who say that they need tension if they are to create are partially right. But that is not the whole story.

In the first place, even if high levels of arousal are needed *during* activity, they are certainly not needed before and after activity. Many people get so excited before an important occasion that they cannot sleep, and similarly they may not be able to sleep afterwards; in both cases the duration of arousal is too long.

Secondly, there must presumably be an ideal amount of arousal for any given situation. If you feel excessively nervous when you walk into a roomful of strangers at a party, you may find that when you go up for an important interview you are incapable of speaking coherently. Many people, in fact, over-react to situations. If over-arousal is really severe, it can lead to complete incapacity for action. More than one examination candidate has reached such a point of tension that he has handed in a totally blank sheet of paper, or has spent the whole examination period signing his name over and over again.

Part of the answer to the stress-creativity problem, then, lies in the concept of fine adjustment. The arousal level needs to be just right—not too little, not too much—and arousal has to last only for as long as it is required. But there is more to it than that. I want to look at the question in a little more detail, because it will lead us to a general principle which seems to me to have very wide implications for the way we ought to be thinking about ourselves and our world.

The Concept of Challenge

There is, I believe, a basic confusion at the heart of the whole stress-creativity argument. The confusion is between stress and challenge. In an earlier chapter, I said that stress is a failure to cope. Now, stress in this sense can never be desirable. Challenge, on the other hand, is a different thing. Challenge by itself does not cause stress; what causes the stress is *failure to cope with the challenge*.

This way of looking at the matter allows us to re-define the terms of the argument. When people talk about the "agony of creation", they do not really mean that *creating* is agony; what is agonizing is the *inability* to create. It is the sitting for hours chewing one's pen that causes the suffering, not the writing. On the contrary, when one is writing well one is happy; it is indeed just this knowledge that makes the inability to write a source of unhappiness.

All this makes perfectly good sense in the light of the principle of fine adjustment. If creation occurs at the moment when the brain reaches balance, it *must* be associated with happiness; similarly, the preceding phase of imbalance, if severe or prolonged, will produce suffering. Now, it is perfectly true that the unrest phase must occur if the cycle is to revolve, but it does not follow that the creativity is proportional to the preceding suffering. If the nervous system is sufficiently finely adjusted, balance will be achieved so rapidly that in effect it will be almost continuous, and hence creative moments will constantly recur. Wide swings between extremes are a sign of instability; the system is not properly adjusted.

The most creative brain, then, will be the one which is most finely adjusted, and a finely adjusted system will not register stress. Stress is a characteristic of an imperfectly balanced system, which is failing to cope with the challenges it has to meet.

The fact remains, however—and this is the germ of truth in the stress-creativity idea—that evolution, both on the individual and the genetic levels, does come about through the surmounting of difficulties. Maharishi certainly recognizes this, but whereas he emphasizes the surmounting (the coming to balance), we often emphasize the preceding phase of turmoil and imbalance.

The relationship between these two phases of evolution is beautifully brought out in the *Bhagavad Gita*. This tells the story of Arjuna, the greatest warrior of his time. He finds himself obliged to fight and kill his relatives, who have gone over to the forces of unrighteousness. To Arjuna this is an insoluble dilemma; his duty as a warrior and defender of righteousness is to fight, but his ethical principles forbid him to kill his kinsmen. He is therefore in a state of acute mental conflict—imbalance—and most of the *Gita* consists in a dialogue on the subject between Arjuna and his charioteer, who is—although Arjuna does not know it at first—Krishna, a divine incarnation.

Arjuna finds himself in a dilemma—in what Gregory Bateson has called a "double bind".[2] A double bind is a situation of acute conflict, in which whatever one does is wrong. Such a situation represents a threat, of course, but also an opportunity, because it is through the *resolution* of double binds that one evolves. In Blake's words, "Without Contraries is no Progression".

In a double-bind situation, one of two things may happen. The first is some form of breakdown. Thus, an experimental neurosis can be induced in dogs which have been trained to respond to a circle but not to an ellipse. If the ellipse is made progressively fatter, so that it becomes more and more similar to a circle, the dogs become frantic in their attempts to distinguish between the two, until eventually they break down.

The solution to the problem would be to abandon the attempt to distinguish between the circle and the ellipse and to resort to simple guessing. But most dogs cannot do this, for to find the solution they would have to put themselves outside the problem, as it were, and to take a "meta-decision" about strategy. A human being can avoid developing a neurosis in the circle-ellipse dilemma because, unlike the dog, he can see the situation in a wider context.

Notice that, for the paradox to "bite", the subject must be intelligent enough but not too intelligent. The dog must be capable of solving the original circle-ellipse problem, otherwise it will not be affected by the dilemma caused by the increasing similarity between the two figures. Similarly, Arjuna's problem was due, indirectly, to his own moral sensibility; had his sensibility been less, he would not have been so troubled by the conflict between different conceptions of duty. Most dramatic literature, of course, deals with conflicts of this general kind.

Another "experimental" situation in which a double-bind situation is deliberately set up to induce neurosis, this time in human beings, is "brainwashing". The prisoner finds himself isolated from everything and everyone he knows. He is constantly exposed to information supplied by his captors; he is alternately cajoled and threatened, pampered and ill-used. The result, in some cases at least, is breakdown followed by a reorientation of the prisoner's opinions on the lines desired by his captors.

However, brainwashing does not always work. Resistance to the process seems to depend on possessing either a very firm character structure or else the ability to see the whole situation in a wider context. That some people have such an ability emerges from the accounts of the Nazi concentration camps in the second world war. In these terrible conditions, many prisoners became dehumanized, and some even co-operated with their torturers. Others, however, did not respond in these ways. There were some—not many, it is true, but some nevertheless—who emerged from the unimaginable ordeal without bitterness and without loss of humanity. Such people seem to have had the ability to integrate even this ultimate in horror into a wider context, and so to succeed in preserving a sense of wholeness and stability.

Here we have the clue to the second possible response to a double-bind situation—resolution. But how can *resolution* occur in a dilemma which is, by definition, insoluble? The answer is, by a shift to a different "level of awareness". According to Maharishi, this is the message of the *Gita*; problems such as Arjuna's cannot be solved on their own level—the level of ordinary thinking—but only by taking the awareness to subtler levels through the practice of yoga—that is, TM.

Now, how are we to understand this talk of levels? When we encounter the idea in the setting of the *Gita*, it is apt to seem a little remote from modern thinking—movingly poetic, perhaps, but not easy to interpret in a 20th-century setting. It seems to me, however, that it is possible to think about levels in an entirely modern way—which, incidentally, has a good deal of relevance to the hierarchical structure of the nervous system which I discussed in Chapter Seven. I suggest that we approach the concept of levels in the light of Bateson's description of "learning" (in the quite general sense of change).

Bateson regards learning as built up of a number of *logical levels*[3]; a most fruitful idea, which I want to borrow with slight modifications. Here it is, in my own words.

Level o learning characterizes an organism (or a machine)

which cannot learn from its experience. All the responses of which it is capable have been built-in from the start. An organism or machine of this kind may behave in very complicated ways, which may even give the impression of "intelligence" if a sufficiently large repertoire has been included by its designer, but the essential feature of Level 0 learning is that experience does not induce any structural changes in the mechanism. A computer which has been programmed to play the best possible game of noughts and crosses would exhibit Level 0 learning, and so would an animal (if there are any such) whose actions were wholly guided by instinct. Descartes' view of animals seemed to imply that they were all automata of this kind.

Level 1 learning occurs when an animal (or machine) learns from its experience. This implies feedback. Structural changes occur in response to experience which affect future behaviour. A burned child dreads the fire. This implies that the sight of flames and the pain of being burned have become associated in the brain through experience. The brain must therefore be capable of change in response to experience. This is the simplest form of real learning, and it probably occurs in all living creatures.

Now, what is Level 2 learning? At this level, the organism gains the ability to look at Level 1 learning "from outside", and to change the *way* in which it learns—that is, to adopt a new Plan for learning. For example, two students are required to learn a large amount of material for an examination. One simply attempts to memorize the facts, while the other tries to order them in his mind in a logical pattern. The second student has made use of Level 2 learning. This means that he has actually learned two things: he has learned the facts required for his examination, and he has learned a *technique for learning* which he can apply in future in other situations. This second form of learning is much the more useful of the two.

In practice, of course, everyone uses the second form to some extent, and a great deal of professional and technical training consists in Level 2 learning; that is, in the acquisition of Plans for arranging facts. Medical students, for example, have to learn a Plan for taking a patient's history, for conducting a physical examination, for looking at a chest X-ray, and so on. To quite a large extent, probably, differences in skill and ability are related to differences in the Plans for learning which people adopt—that is, to differences in the efficiency of their Level 2 learning.

Much of what we call "character" is also based on Level 2 learning. When we say of someone that he is mean, or brave, or jealous, we mean that he will behave in particular ways in certain situations. Traits refer to acquired reaction patterns (Plans) which are learned (usually in childhood). Neuroses could be regarded as faulty patterns of Level 2 learning.

It is remarkably difficult to change a Level 2 pattern. A good example of this is provided by superstition. If someone believes that to see a black cat is unlucky, no amount of argument, no accumulation of contrary instances, will persuade him otherwise. For if the sighting of such an animal is followed by mischance, he will count this as confirmation of the superstition, while if it is not he will ascribe his fortunate escape to the use of some apotropaic ritual, such as touching wood. Magical thinking, in fact, is self-fulfilling; it is based on a "heads I win, tails you lose" principle.

Even to shift from one kind of Level 2 thinking to another does not imply a move to Level 3. Thus, the drunkard who attends a temperance meeting and becomes a teetotaller overnight has remained at Level 2, but has reversed the pattern. (For this reason, there is always a strong possibility that backsliding will occur, through a second reversal.) Many religious conversions are of this kind. They could be compared to the change in perspective which occurs when one stares for some time at a Necker cube (fig. 10).

Level 3 learning is much more difficult to achieve, and therefore comparatively rare. Just as Level 2 learning consists in a reorganization of the way in which Level 1 learning occurs, so Level 3 learning consists in a reorganization of the ways in which Level 2 learning occurs. But since, as we have seen, most of what we usually think of as our personality is based on Level 2 learning patterns, Level 3 learning must necessarily entail a profound reshaping of the self, with a shift of the centre of psychological gravity away from the various traits which formerly made up the self. In terms of the Necker cube analogy, achieving Level 3 learning would be like acquiring the ability to see both perspectives simultaneously.

The liberation from "bondage", from "identification", which is the theme of the *Gita* (and of much Eastern teaching)

FIGURE 10 Necker Cube

seems to consist in achieving this form of learning. At the beginning of the story, Arjuna is in conflict because he is torn between two mutually contradictory concepts of duty. As Krishna unfolds the philosophy of action to him, however, he comes to see that the conflict is only apparent, because he is not really the author of action; action is not produced by the "I", but by the forces of Nature. (See Chapter Fourteen for further discussion of this idea.)

According to Maharishi, such a realization cannot come about through intellectual analysis, but depends on a shift in the level of awareness, and this, as I have said, is to be produced by "transcending". TM must therefore be regarded as a technique for facilitating transition to Level 3 learning.

To summarize: I am suggesting that creativity (in human beings) is the ability to generate new patterns of Level 2 learning by shifting to Level 3. The acquisition of this ability results from the confronting of double-bind situations, and this is the justification for the idea that stress is linked with creativity. But stress does not *produce* creativity. Stress is a symptom of *lack* of creativity; it shows that the shift to Level 3 learning has failed to occur—that the cycle of differentiation has remained in the "imbalance" phase.

The truly creative individual is the one who has this ability to shift, even temporarily, to Level 3 thinking. This does not mean that the genius has no capacity to operate at lower logical levels, such as Level 2; on the contrary, he must be able to bridge the gap and communicate in this way, otherwise he will not be truly creative. The reason that we speak of inspiration is that, in the creative process, insights which are natural at a higher logical level in the hierarchy are brought down to a lower level to be used there. It is quite natural that these insights should often sound paradoxical, precisely because they have arisen through the uniting of opposites, the bringing together of ideas which are incompatible at a lower level. This is the reason for the "ineffability" of mystical experience. The experience is not indescribable, but it sounds violently contradictory. The world is said to be simultaneously many and one, for example, or the mystic speaks of a "shining darkness".

Level 3 thinking is *qualitatively* different from Level 2 thinking. It is in a different dimension; Level 3 thinking is related to Level 2 thinking rather as a sphere is related to a circle.

Logical Levels of Thinking and the Different Levels of Awareness

There are some parallels between the concept of different logical levels of learning (or thinking) and Maharishi's scheme of different levels of awareness which, I am sure, are more than accidental. For Bateson, the shift from a lower logical level to a higher one comes about through a double bind, a paradox which is insoluble on that level and can be resolved only by a shift to a higher level. Now, as I have pointed out in *Seven States of Consciousness*,[4] paradoxicality is a basic feature of all mystical experience. This is specially true of highest-level mysticism, which seems to consist in perceiving that the world is simultaneously many and one. This experience is described in the Upanishads, in the Taoist and Sufi literature, and by certain Western mystics, notably Meister Eckhart.

As I have explained in Chapter Two, it is also the culmination of Maharishi's scheme of "evolution". Indeed, the whole span of development which he describes could be seen in terms of the successive recognition and resolution of paradoxes, or double binds. Each successive state can be seen as a resolution of the paradox of the preceding state. For example, in the fifth state, permanent Self-awareness, the Self is perceived as separate from activity and yet activity continues. This is certainly paradoxical, and indeed Maharishi says that, in the early stages, before it is fully established, dawning enlightenment may feel strange. In the state of full enlightenment, the paradox is resolved, because then the Self is found to be present on both the inner level *and* the outer.

Double binds—contradictions—may thus occur on the path to enlightenment, and, if not resolved, probably play a part in the production of those states of unhappiness and despair which St John of the Cross called the "dark night of the soul". Earlier spiritual masters have often deliberately induced double-bind situations to enhance the progress of their disciples. There are many stories, especially in Sufism and in the Indian and Buddhist traditions, of pupils being repeatedly sent away by their teachers, until at last, often after many years, they were accepted and gained enlightenment. The school which has perhaps made the most systematic use of the double bind is the Zen sect which employs *koans*. The *koan* is a riddle to which there is no answer.* The pupil is instructed to ponder the riddle he has been given continuously, without respite; he must wrestle with it night and day. The result, it seems, is an eventual breakdown of Level 2 thinking, and—if all goes well—a flash of *satori*—a shift to Level 3 thinking, at which the opposites are not resolved but are included in a larger, more comprehensive, whole.

Maharishi's technique is, of course, quite different, at least on the surface. Maharishi strongly disputes the view that "life is a struggle" and that suffering is necessary for progress. Yet my own impression—and I must emphasize that this is a personal view—is that Blake's "Without Contraries is no Progression" is implicit in SCI. This does not mean that suffering is a

---

* The riddle which the Mad Hatter propounds to Alice—why is a raven like a writing desk?—is a perfect example of a *koan*.

good thing; but it does mean that resolution of tensions by the transcending of contradictions seems to be at the root of all evolution, biological and individual. And TM is concerned with this resolution. It is like lubricating oil, which helps in the readjusting process and so facilitates the course of evolution.

It is interesting that Bateson finds himself led by his analysis of learning to speculate on lines which can only be described as mystical. Lower animals such as planarian worms, he suggests, probably cannot go beyond Level 1 learning. Mammals other than man are probably capable of Level 2 learning but not of Level 3, while human beings can sometimes achieve Level 3. If they do, they may reach a state in which "the identified self is no longer in charge of organizing behaviour". (This sounds remarkably like Maharishi's fifth state.) Alternatively:

> For others, more creative, the resolution of contraries reveals a world in which personal identity merges into all the processes of relationship in some vast ecology or aesthetics of cosmic interaction. That any of these can survive seems almost miraculous, but some are perhaps saved from being swept away by their ability to focus on the minutiae of life. Every detail of the universe is seen as proposing a view of the whole.[5]

What Bateson seems to be feeling after here is the state of full enlightenment. I am tempted to speculate that this develops as the result of yet another shift, this time from Level 3 to Level 4. Bateson believes that this shift does not occur in any creature on earth (although he does point out that the fact that evolution has produced creatures [ourselves] which are capable of Level 3 learning means that evolution has achieved Level 4 learning). But is he right in this? Maharishi's division of individual evolution into two phases, the first affecting inner awareness and the second outer perception, seems to suggest that a shift to Level 4 may indeed occur. At any rate, it is an intriguing thought.

Conclusion

The idea that creativity occurs through the transcending of double binds seems to me a most fruitful one. In particular, it helps to bring out the close interrelationships which, I believe, exist among creativity, evolution, and mystical experience.

In Part IV, I shall explore the significance of these interrelationships in more detail.

PART FOUR

XII

Man and the Universe

IN A RECENT documentary television programme about the Pygmies of Africa, the anthropologist Colin Turnbull described the extraordinary relation of these remarkable people to their forest. The forest supplies the Pygmies with everything they need—food, drink, shelter—and the Pygmies in turn react to it as if it were a person. When they travel through it, they call out "Father! Mother!" as they go. Turnbull relates how he awoke, one moonlit night, to hear the sound of singing. Not far away he found a Pygmy friend of his in a clearing by himself, dancing and singing. When Turnbull asked him what he was doing, he replied that he was singing to the forest.

One could not ask for a better example of what the anthropologist L. Lévy-Bruhl has called "participation mystique". It seems possible that the myth of a Golden Age, a lost paradise, a Garden of Eden, which one finds in so many cultures across the world, may derive from racial memories of a time when all human beings were hunters and gatherers rather than agriculturalists. It is easy to sentimentalize, and I do not want to revive Rousseauesque ideas of the Noble Savage, but the reports of anthropologists who have studied a wide range of pre-agricultural communities in different parts of the world do suggest that when human beings took what Nature had to offer without trying to manipulate her they had a sense of belonging and unity which they have seldom managed to recapture subsequently.

The whole trend of civilization, especially in the last 300 years or so, has been away from "participation mystique". Man "conquers Nature" (unmindful of the maxim, proposed by Gregory Bateson, that "the creature which wins against its environment destroys itself"). And of course the method works; up to a point, anyway. We have proved it by going to the moon. But there is a price to pay, in the shape of a sense of alienation. For the scientific world view implies—or at least is

usually taken to imply—a view of life which is fundamentally
nihilistic. Life "has no meaning"; it is a cosmic accident, and
we are cast adrift on an island in space without hope of rescue.
There is no sense to be found in Nature, no purpose, and to
look to her for any kind of justification for our ethical values
is a waste of time.

So general is this attitude today that it is difficult to give
specific instances of it, but a particularly clear expression is to
be found in Jacques Monod's *Chance and Necessity*. In this book,
as in a host of others, we are exhorted to accept the reality of
our isolation. If we delude ourselves by believing otherwise we
merely build up a dishonest attitude which ultimately vitiates
all our thinking and behaviour.

In the past, people have usually found a sense of belonging
through religion. Today, almost all religions are losing ground
rapidly, but at a popular level science and religion have cross-
bred to produce odd hybrids, such as the belief that visitors
from space have brought us knowledge from time to time and
are still doing so today, landing on earth in UFOs and com-
municating with favoured individuals.* Books purporting to
prove the truth of these ideas through surveys of archaeological
remains in Egypt, South America, and elsewhere are currently
enjoying enormous sales, and it is easy to see why. Gods in
chariots are no longer credible; superhumanly intelligent (and
benevolent) visitors in UFOs are. If the universe is populated
by numerous civilizations, many more highly developed than
our own, and if these are watching over us and taking care of
us, ready to protect us against the consequences of our own
folly, we are no longer alone; we belong, we have been rescued.

To laugh at these ideas, or to seek to prove their insubstan-
tiality, is to miss the essential point, which is precisely this need
to feel oneself a part of the Whole. And *that* need is by no means
confined to the naive and unsophisticated. It is, if you like,
"mystical", but it is the root not only of art but of science too.

Not long ago I saw a television film of a group of young
physicists in America, performing a dawn ceremony of "sun
worship", in which they expressed their sense of unity with,

* I must admit that these ideas seem to me purely fantastic.
However, at least one eminent contemporary scientist, John Taylor,
Professor of Mathematics at King's College, London, takes them
seriously. (See his book *Black Holes*, Fontana, 1974, pp. 32–34.)

and gratitude to, the source of life in the solar system. A senior British scientist, commenting on the film, remarked that to him these people seemed barmy—pleasantly barmy, perhaps, but barmy none the less. The contrast in attitudes is most instructive.

To me, one of the most hopeful features of our present intellectual climate is the increasing realization of the need to relate man to the universe, and to recover, if possible, the sense of "participation mystique".

Now, if this awareness of a lack were merely on the emotional level it would still be important, for it would point to a psychological need which demands fulfilment in some way and which might cause disturbance if left unfulfilled. But there is today a still undefined but powerful groundswell of ideas within science itself which suggests that the whole "castaway in space" view of man is mistaken. That view is beginning to look like a survival of nineteenth-century scientific thought-patterns, which fail to take account of modern developments and, particularly, of cybernetics. There are today a large number of biologists, evolutionists, psychologists and others who are thinking about life and man in terms which relate rather than divide. What I want to do in this final part of the book is to apply this way of thinking, in the light of SCI, to the view of the brain which I developed in the earlier chapters. It is only fair to warn you that we shall rapidly find ourselves sailing into very deep waters, and no doubt there will be some readers who will feel that I should have done better to be more cautious. I think, however, that not to follow these ideas as far as they seem to lead us would be a pity; even if I come to grief on the way, the journey may none the less be an interesting one.

The theme I want to consider is the relation between man and the universe. In both East and West, we find a long tradition of belief that man and the universe somehow mirror each other, and in earlier times this led to a concept of man as microcosm and of the universe as an organism. It is an easy idea to make fun of today; and in its crude form it is, no doubt, ridiculous. And yet, I wonder whether modern science is not leading us back towards a restatement of this ancient doctrine. At any rate, the possibility will, I think, repay further examination.

Cybernetics, Man, and Nature[1]

So far in this book I have been concentrating almost wholly on the individual, and treating the mind as if it were confined within the boundaries of the skin. But this is only a manner of speaking; mind and brain are not synonymous. This is true whatever view one takes of the mind-body problem.

Consider a potter who is making a free sculptural form. At first, perhaps, she has almost no idea, at least consciously, of what it will be. She takes the clay and begins to mould it almost at random. Gradually a shape begins to emerge, and this initial impulse decides the direction the work will take. A constant interchange then goes on between hands and eyes via the brain until, eventually, the form is complete.

What we have here is essentially a feedback process. A loop has

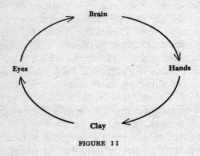

FIGURE 11

been set up, consisting of brain—hands—clay—eyes—brain.* I will draw it, to emphasize the point that it has no beginning or end (fig. 11). It is like a round robin; no single component is at its head.

Now, where, in this context, is the mind? To this question most modern neuropsychologists would answer that the mind *is* the brain. But this will not do *even in materialistic terms*. According to science itself, the brain is a mechanism, and the current hypothesis is that it is a cybernetic mechanism—as we saw in Chapter Six, this was the reason Wiener gave for dismissing

* There is also a shorter but important loop involving brain-hands-clay-brain, but I have omitted this from the discussion for the sake of clarity.

the vitalist-mechanist controversy. In practical terms, this means that the brain is made up of hierarchies of feedback loops which interact to give the effect of purpose. So far so good; but, as I have just pointed out, the loops are not confined to the brain; they pass outside it, into the environment. For the potter, the clay she is moulding is part of the total thinking process. Hence, the mind cannot be just the brain, but must be the brain *plus* the environment. In other words, if you invoke cybernetics to solve the mind-body problem, you are compelled to widen your concept of mind immeasurably.

For the figure I have drawn to illustrate the process of sculpting clay does not by any means exhaust the range of mind —indeed, it does not even begin to convey its extent. The number of influences which may help to shape the form the potter makes is almost infinite. Memories of previous forms seen, ideas, dreams, and all the multifarious factors which go to make up personality are concerned, and so mind turns out to extend not only in the dimension of space but also in that of time. Our brains are not isolated from the rest of time and space, but are more like knots in a net, or like local eddies in a sea full of currents.

The notion of the "individual mind" is comparable to that of the atom. For nineteenth-century physicists, atoms were what their name implies—essentially unchangeable and indestructible. Subsequent research has yielded a very different picture. Today, physicists paint a far more fluid picture of the world, and seem to regard the particles they study as local manifestations or concentrations of energy, which appear and disappear in space like wrinkles in a sheet.

I think we should look at the notion of mind in much the same way. To try to isolate a mind is like trying to obtain a single magnetic pole by cutting a magnet into smaller and smaller pieces; it cannot be done. The mind has no boundaries; it stretches out in space and time illimitably. If we do draw boundaries, it is merely a matter of convenience; they have no real existence.

Suppose a child asks you to show her the Aegean sea on the map. You do so, and then she asks where is the Mediterranean. You point that out also. "But the Aegean seems to be part of the Mediterranean," she objects. "Well, so it is in a way," you say. "But where is the dividing line between them?" "There isn't one," you reply; "it's just a matter of convenience to give different names to different parts of the same piece of water."

So with the mind; for some purposes it is convenient to draw the boundary at the skin, but for others it is totally misleading to do so. As Gregory Bateson has put it: "The individual mind is immanent but not only in the body. It is immanent also in pathways and messages outside the body; and there is a larger Mind of which the individual mind is only a subsystem."[2]

This idea of a "larger Mind" is one I shall take up a little later. For the present, let us look a little more closely at the question of "pathways and messages".

This approach can easily be applied to the mechanism of temperature regulation which I discussed in Chapter Six. A good deal of temperature regulation is related to feedback loops within the body—metabolic pathways running via the thyroid gland and hypothalamus, and so on. But information from the *outer* world also affects the system. Here we encounter quite lengthy loops. Suppose, for example, you wake up one morning and see that it is snowing outside; this visual information makes you throw some logs on the fire. You have not waited for a fall in temperature to make you feel cold; you have anticipated the situation by reacting to a visual cue. The mechanism concerned is still a homeostatic one, but it is at a high level.

The cybernetic view of the mind suggests a model which is rather analogous to the contour lines on a map. These lines, of course, join together areas of land at the same height above sea level, and so naturally they never break off; if you follow them far enough they always ultimately form loops. In much the same way one could draw feedback loops for the mind, representing sequences of events at the same logical level in the hierarchy; and these, too, would never break off provided they were followed far enough. *What we call a mind is simply a localized concentration of such loops.*

The unity of mind is a relative affair. Internally, it is possible for semi-separate subsystems of loops to form, like eddies within eddies, and these may give rise, in extreme cases, to "multiple personalities", in which two—very rarely more than two— personalities apparently occupy the same body alternately. In less extreme and dramatic form, such subsystems produce the various facets of personality which all of us possess, so that we may be almost totally different people at home and in the office.

Externally, the loops extend in time and space far beyond what we can consciously recognize. In the cortex of our brain we store the information we have accumulated in our lifetime, but that information may arise from the whole span of history. Your actions, for instance, may be in part influenced by what Plato thought and said over 2,000 years ago. But the information stored in the older parts of the brain—in the core—is far more ancient than that. It is concerned with the most basic activities of life—eating, sleeping, mating, fighting, running away—and it was laid down long before man evolved, and even before the mammals appeared.

As with time, so with space. Today we know that our earth is not totally isolated in a void; "empty" space has turned out to be filled with radiations and streaming particles, and more and more evidence is accumulating to show that living creatures probably including ourselves, respond to cosmic rhythms of the sun and moon and, perhaps, of the universe as a whole.[3]

Such discoveries have immense relevance to the question of our relation to the rest of the cosmos. If mind is so much part of the universe as the cybernetic approach implies, the whole idea of "man against Nature" must be mistaken. We are part of Nature, whether we like it or not, and to call an action unnatural makes no sense; everything we think or do is ultimately natural. This conclusion is comforting in some ways, but not so comforting in others; the dinosaurs too were products of Nature. However, it does at least help us to get human concerns into some sort of perspective. The real significance of the cybernetic, integrative approach is that it points the way to an ultimate reconciliation between science and the human desire for a sense of belonging which has up to now found expression in religion. We are not there yet; but at least it seems possible that we are moving in the right direction. Let me try to show why this is so.

The Quest for the Source

Perhaps the greatest puzzle facing biologists today is the question, where does all the organization come from? In his justly celebrated book *What is Life?* the physicist Erwin Schrödinger brought this point out clearly.[4] What distinguishes living systems from non-living is that they maintain, or even (during growth) increase, their internal *orderliness*.

In general, orderly systems tend to break down in time into less orderly ones. For example, untended buildings tend to crumble into ruins; motor cars left out in the weather without attention rust away; the contents of drawers become more and more untidy unless you make a definite effort to arrange them. By the same token, order does not commonly emerge spontaneously from disorder. If you take a set of watch parts and shake them up for a while in a box, you do not expect that when you open the box you will find a complete watch ticking away and showing the correct time. Theoretically it is not totally impossible that this should happen, but it is almost infinitely unlikely.

The physicists' name for disorder is "entropy". According to the famous Second Law of Thermodynamics, all "closed" systems—that is, systems which are functionally isolated from the rest of the universe—tend to increase their entropy. This law holds good so far as we know, and some cosmologists have applied it to the universe as a whole and have predicted that the universe must eventually reach a stage of total inertness, like a run-down clock, in which entropy is at a maximum. This idea has, however, been challenged, and there seems no way in which we can know whether the laws that hold good for us here on earth can be applied to the universe as a whole.

At first glance, living organisms seem to form an exception to the general rule that entropy must increase. During growth, an organism is constantly taking material into itself and using it to build its own structure. Once growth is completed, the organism maintains a balance between income and expenditure, and this is crucial to life. In disease and in senescence the balance is disturbed, and at death it finally tips over in the direction of disorder. Within a short space of time, all the complex structure of the body breaks down, and orderliness gives way to disorder.

But although disorder wins in the end, the fact remains that for long periods—some 70 years in our own case, hundreds of years in the case of certain kinds of tree—the Second Law of Thermodynamics is apparently in abeyance. This is very puzzling, because the Second Law is supposed to be as inexorable as the laws of the Medes and Persians. Do organisms really disobey it?

The short answer is, no. As we saw in Chapter Four, organisms are not "closed" but are "open". They exchange material with their surroundings, and so do not "come within the meaning of the Act" so far as the Second Law is concerned.

But does that finally dispose of the problem? Again, the answer is no. Let us look at it a little more closely.

Life is essentially dynamic. Organisms achieve relative stability, but their stability is dynamic. A block of concrete lying on the ground is stable, but its stability is of a different order from that of a spinning top. The block of concrete will rest happily on any of its six faces, but not on one corner. The spinning top, on the other hand, will maintain any position *so long as it is spinning*. The stability of the top, though provisional and temporary, is more adaptable and "interesting" than that of the block of concrete. Organisms are like tops; or, to change the metaphor, they are like jugglers, constantly keeping up a dazzling display of skill in the face of apparent probability. How do they do it?

The process by which organisms maintain themselves alive is called metabolism. Literally, this means exchange. But what is exchanged?

It might seem that the obvious answer is material. We eat and excrete, we breathe oxygen in and carbon dioxide out, and in doing these things we are constantly exchanging material with our surroundings. But, as Schrödinger emphasizes, the exchange of *material* is not the real significance of metabolism. What organisms really require from their surroundings is *order*.

Except for the most primitive living forms, all creatures are composed chiefly of three kinds of material—carbohydrates, fats (and fat-like substances), and proteins. All these are *orderly* arrangements of atoms. Animals, unlike plants, cannot build them up from scratch but can only reorganize ready-made components which they obtain, ultimately, from plants. This is specially true of proteins, which are perhaps the most important kind of substance found in living creatures. Proteins are very large molecules, which are made up of chains of amino acids. Animals can break down the proteins they eat into their component amino acids and can shuffle these around to make

new proteins, but they cannot themselves make amino acids—
at least, not the so-called essential amino acids; some other
kinds can be built up from fragments. Only plants can synthe-
size complex molecules from their elements; plants are therefore like factories which construct the essential components
needed by other manufacturers.

The construction process requires energy, which plants
obtain from sunlight. Thus, in tracing the chain of causation
back we have already been led outside the boundaries of our
planet, and if we go on to ask where the sun gets its energy
from, we are taken outside the solar system altogether and
must consider the way in which stars are thought to evolve
from masses of interstellar gas, which may itself have formed
part of earlier stars long dead and broken up. Go back still
further, and you are brought up against the question of the
origin of the universe itself.

But it is not necessary to go back so far in time to discover
profound questions about the origin of order. Such problems
are intimately bound up with the puzzle of the origin of life.
It is true that many biologists believe life to have originated
through the random mixing of suitable molecules on the primitive earth, and experiments have shown that it is possible to
obtain amino acids in this way in circumstances similar to
those supposed to have existed on earth at the presumed time
of the origin of life. But evidently a mixture of amino acids
does not constitute a living cell, any more than a collection of
clock parts constitutes a clock. In both cases something else is
needed, and that is *order*.

A cell is a very complex structure, and is not merely a bag
of proteins, carbohydrates, fats, and so on. It contains a large
number of parts and "organelles", which must all function
together harmoniously if the cell is to work. The real challenge
to evolutionary biology is to account for this astonishing
complexity. As one biologist, Peter T. Mora, has put it:

Biochemists will agree that we are very far from knowing
how this interrelationship and control comes about in space
and time, and we do not, at least not yet, foresee the synthesis
of a functioning, living unit from a molecular level. Claim
to the contrary comes from insufficient biochemical knowledge or from a belief that the present molecular biology

will supply the information imminently. This last tenet is exactly what I am questioning. Characteristically, such claims come more frequently from physicists or chemists who examine biological macromolecules, than from biochemists, and scarcely ever from those biologists who work with a small living unit, such as a cell.[5]

I must be careful at this point to avoid seeming to postulate a "God of the gaps". I am not saying that, because we do not understand how life originated, we must therefore believe in a demiurge or a *deus ex machina*. What I am saying is that we should recognize that the universe is unimaginably complex and that an understanding of the nature of life, and hence of ourselves, will not come until we have learned more about these deeper aspects.

As Mora points out in the article from which I have quoted, life, at all stages of evolution and not merely at its origin, is permeated with *purpose*. Teleological explanations are out of fashion at present, largely for historical reasons; it has taken science a long time to break free from the metaphysical assumptions of the Middle Ages (in which purpose was a central notion) and to construct an "objective" approach to the study of the natural world. But to rule out consideration of purpose from biology, Mora believes, is to blind oneself to the obvious.

The great task which faces biologists is to explain, not only how life originated, but why, having done so, it became more and more complex and produced ever higher forms. What is the source of the enormous and profligate variety of Nature?

One answer—which has been forcefully argued by Jacques Monod in *Chance and Necessity*—is to say that the driving force in evolution is chance. Randomly occurring mutations throw up variations at hazard, and these are then shaped by the environment into the species we actually see. Because the occurrence of a mutation (that is, a change in the structure of DNA, the genetic material) is essentially unpredictable (since it is caused by a quantum event), and because the *effects* of a given mutation on the body are also unpredictable, we cannot, Monod argues, offer any scientific justification for belief in the existence of a "plan" in nature. We are contingent beings. As it happens, we exist; but we might equally well not have done so.

Here we find the train of thought which began with the Copernican revolution brought to its logical conclusion. In the Middle Ages, the earth was thought to be at the centre of the universe. This did not mean, as is often supposed, that it was therefore valuable or important—on the contrary, it was the lowliest part of creation—but at least it belonged; it had a place in the scheme of things. Subsequent astronomical discoveries have shown our earth to be more and more contingent, until today we know it is merely one of several planets revolving round a not very impressive star in an outlying part of a run-of-the-mill galaxy, which itself is merely one of an uncountable swarm of galaxies in a universe whose dimensions we cannot comprehend.

After Copernicus, the next shaker of our self-confidence was Darwin, who showed that the myth of a special creation of Man to rule the animals was just that—a myth. Instead, we are ourselves animals who have achieved a dubious and quite probably short-lived ascendancy simply as the result of blind "natural selection".

And now, biochemists such as James Watson and Francis Crick and their successors have shown that the secret of life is based on quite simple physico-chemical events which, Monod assures us, are at the mercy of chance.

We have, it seems, reached rock-bottom at last. Perhaps it is time to return to the surface. What, if anything, can be said on the other side?

First of all, the basic mechanism of genetics is not settled once and for all; nothing in science ever is. At present it is an axiom of biology that the experiences of one generation are not passed on to the next; there is no feedback from experience to germ cells. If this were one day found not to be so, the whole picture would change. Monod regards this as "inconceivable", but, as Sir Peter Medawar pointed out in a recent radio discussion with Monod, such sweeping assertions are dangerous; the great physiologist J. S. Haldane believed, many years ago, that the existence of a compound like DNA was inconceivable.

Secondly, the whole question of what we mean by "chance" and "randomness" is a profoundly difficult one, which has intrigued some of the greatest minds in physics. Wolfgang Pauli, for example, believed in the existence of acausal patterns linking random events and giving rise to apparently meaningful coincidence. In his book *The Roots of Coincidences*, Arthur Koestler quotes Pauli as saying that, since the introduction of Heisenberg's uncertainty principle, physics has had to "renounce its proud claim to understand the *whole* of the world. But this predicament may contain the seed of further developments* which will correct the previous one-sided orientation and will move towards a unitary world-view in which science is only part of the whole."[6]

Here we are coming close to the heart of the problem. The whole trend of science over the last 300 years has been towards an ideal of objectivity. Our feelings, our preferences, should not dictate the way in which we understand the world; if we allow them to do so we shall be led astray.

Now, the objectivist principle has worked magnificently in relation to the physical world; it has achieved remarkably little in relation to the mental one. Above all, it has led us to a position where we feel ourselves to be outside Nature, separate from the rest of the universe. But this *must* be wrong. We have been produced by the universe, we are part of it, and we cannot be outside it. What has happened?

At this point we reach the boundaries of present scientific thought, and begin to enter the realm of metaphysics. The difference between the "reductionists" and their opponents seems to be, in part at least, a matter of temperament. Some people seem instinctively to want to dissect the world into smaller and smaller pieces so as to understand it better, while others want to try to relate what they already know to the larger whole. One approach leads to science as we have known it in the last 300 years or so, while the other perhaps points the direction thought will increasingly take in the future. This is not to say that the reductionist approach is of no value; on the contrary, it is immensely powerful and effective for its specific purpose. The mistake is to think that it is the only path to knowledge. Cybernetic ideas, when applied to biology and evolution, seem to point a way in which science may be able to integrate as well as to divide, and this seems to me profoundly exciting.

Ludwig Von Bertalanffy, as well as a number of other highly respected biologists and evolutionists, such as C. H. Wadding-

* Notice the implied reference to the cycle of differentiation!

ton, have developed ideas of evolution based on an "organismic" conception of the universe, which have been given the imposing name "General Systems Theory". Some interesting implications of this approach are to be found in *Beyond Reductionism*, edited by Arthur Koestler and J. R. Smythies. I cannot even begin to summarize these ideas here. What I should like to do instead is to offer a scientific parable to illustrate the feeling I have about where the new way of thinking seems to be leading us.

If you go any day to the Science Museum in London, you will find an experiment in progress. A large pendulum is set swinging along the north-south axis each day at noon. If you return some hours later, you will find that it is no longer swinging along this axis, but is some degrees off. The reason, of course, is the rotation of the earth, which has continued while the pendulum went on swinging in the direction in which it was first started. If the experiment were carried out at the North or South pole, the pendulum would appear to make a complete revolution in twenty-four hours, but even at our latitude the effect is quite perceptible.

This all seems simple enough until one really begins to think about it. For it is a fundamental of Einstein's theory of relativity that motion is relative; thus, although we normally think of the earth as revolving on its axis, we are entitled, if we wish, to say that the earth remains still and the rest of the universe revolves around it. According to the theory, there is no way of distinguishing between these two descriptions of the situation.

The odd thing is, however, that the pendulum seems able to distinguish between them. If we do say that the earth has remained still while the universe revolves, it seems that we must explain the rotation of the pendulum by saying that it is due to the rotation of the universe.

This is in fact what Ernst Mach did say in his famous Principle, which implies that the inertia of the pendulum (that is, its tendency to continue swinging in the direction in which it was started), and indeed, the inertia of all bodies on the earth and elsewhere, is produced by the rotation of the fixed stars. To some scientists and philosophers (such as Bertrand Russell) this idea smacks of astrology, and Mach's Principle is still a subject of contention. However, it seems at present to be the most widely favoured explanation of inertia, and it played a large part in Einstein's thought. If it is correct, it is a most surprising idea, for it means that one of the most basic features of our experience—the resistance one feels when one moves an object horizontally, the force which one feels when one tries to stop a horizontally moving object, whether it is a bus or a bullet —is due to the mass of the fixed stars. In other words, the behaviour of objects on earth cannot be understood *without reference to the universe as a whole*.[7]

Now, I think that we may well one day discover a Mach's Principle of evolution. We shall find laws linking evolution on this earth with the laws governing the cosmos as a whole, and when we have done so we shall see that the ancient intuition of "plan" did have a meaning after all. The problem is, however, that if we are capable of discovering these laws at all it will take a very long time, and meanwhile we need to conduct our lives in a way which will not bring about disaster. Is there, then, a short cut to understanding?

Throughout history, there have been people who have claimed to perceive cosmic relationships of the kind I have postulated. In the West we call such people mystics, which is usually a derogatory term. In the East they achieved greater social recognition and approval, and in India and China particularly there grew up great systems of thought based upon mystical experience. The essential feature of all such experience is that it looks for knowledge, not primarily in the outer world, through the senses, but in the inner world of the mind. The claim of the mystics, at all times and in all cultures, is that they have attained direct knowledge of the Source. What are the main features of the world-view which their experience gave rise to?

Let us begin in China. For the Taoists, the ever-changing phenomena of life reflect the swirling currents within the Tao (an untranslatable term), which was conceived of as changeless and ever-changing at the same time. The Tao both gave rise to all the manifest world and gave rise to nothing. What is implied here is a view of the world which differs radically from that current in the West in the nineteenth century but which is coming to seem more and more acceptable in the second half of the twentieth.

In the West we have typically thought of the world as composed of things. On the physical level, there are the tables and chairs so often unimaginatively cited as "objects" by

6•

philosophers; there are also elephants and pumpkins, stars and cheese mites, false teeth and oak trees—all more or less separable from one another as identifiable items. Even on the mental level, we instinctively adopt the same approach: we speak of the mind as containing "ideas", and we describe people as exhibiting identifiable characteristics like meanness, courage, honesty and so on. To people who think in this way, it is natural to suppose that the various things we see and touch can be manipulated to serve our wills; to regard ourselves as separate from the world. This is the root of the myth of objectivity.

For the Taoists, on the other hand, this way of looking at the matter is no more than a convenience; it does not express the truth.

[Taoism] recognizes that, though fixed concepts referring to things and states can be extracted by human thought from the mobile reality, and can be useful, there is actually no way of reconstructing the mobility of the real by adding up fixed concepts. Therefore the most important element—the only element that matters—is always left out of the ordinary ideas most of us have, on which we base our worlds and with which we try to come to terms with them. All static conceptualism is in the last resort impotent. For even our most sophisticated cosmological reasoning arises from, and leads back to, integral concepts which have this enormous primary fallacy built into them. The Tao which Taoism knows . . . is a seamless web of unbroken movement and change, filled with undulations, waves, patterns of ripples and temporary "standing waves" like a river.[8]

The astonishing similarity between Taoist thought and the most modern scientific theories about matter and life has been emphasized by Joseph Needham. Certainly the Taoist world-view seems to have much in common with cybernetics. It implies the notion of *pattern*, which enfolds not only life within our society and on this planet but also the furthest reaches of the cosmos in space and time; and this, I submit, is the world-view to which we in the West are being inexorably led by the logic of our own discoveries. The nineteenth-century billiard-ball model of the atom, like the concept of the individual, has been shown to be untenable, and instead we live in a world of constant flow and change. Matter and life, in fact, turn out to be much less like a collection of things and much more like ripples on the Tao.*

We find this same idea, though perhaps less explicitly worked out, in the Indian concept of the three *gunas*—the three strands or forces which are supposed to interweave to give rise to the whole phenomenal world, including the world of mind. This is essentially a dynamic, fluid view of Nature, which seems to imply an outlook very similar, at least in fundamentals, to that of Taoism.

There is another aspect of the Chinese and Indian world pictures which needs to be mentioned, and that is their foundation in paradox. In China the Tao, and in India Brahman, were regarded as the impersonal Source of everything that exists; at the same time, however, both were said to be inactive. The basic paradox is thus that the Tao or Brahman gives rise to the world, yet nothing happens to it at all. This root paradox generates many others, as we see in this passage from *Chuang Tzu*.

> The Tao has reality and evidence, but no action and no form. It may be transmitted but it cannot be received. It may be attained but cannot be seen. It exists by and through itself. It existed before Heaven and Earth, and indeed for all eternity. It causes the gods to be divine and the world to be produced. It is above the zenith, but it is not high. It is beneath the nadir but it is not low. Though prior to heaven and earth it is not ancient. Though older than the most ancient, it is not old.[9]

* Bertrand Russell makes what is essentially the same point:

"things" have been invented by human beings for their own convenience. This is not obvious on the earth's surface because, owing to the low temperature, there is a certain degree of apparent stability. But it would be obvious if one could live on the sun where there is nothing but perpetually changing whirlwinds of gas. If you lived on the sun, you would never have formed the idea of "things", and you would never have thought of counting because there would be nothing to count. (*Portraits from Memory*, pp. 41–42.)

Very similar paradoxes are found over and over again in the Upanishads. Thus, the Isa Upanishad says: "The Spirit, without moving, is swifter than the mind. . . . Standing still, he overtakes those who run . . . He moves, and moves not.[10] And Maharishi's teaching follows this tradition.

> The unbounded field of Being [Brahman] ranges from the unmanifested, absolute, eternal state to the gross, relative, ever-changing states of phenomenal life in the same way as the ocean ranges from eternal silence at its bottom to the great activity of perpetually moving waves on the surface. One extremity is eternally silent, never-changing in its nature, the other is active and ever-changing.
>
> Both these states, the relative and the absolute, are the states of Being. Being is eternal, never-changing in Its absolute state and eternally ever-changing in Its relative states. Remaining ever in Its omnipresent, absolute status, It is found to be in the ever-changing phases of phenomenal existence and relative creation. The entire field of life, from the individual to the cosmos, is nothing but the expression of eternal, absolute, never-changing, omnipresent Being in the relative, ever-changing phases of existence.[11]

In the Western tradition we find the same idea, though less frequently and usually less explicitly. What is probably the earliest Western reference to it is in the writings of Heraclitus, who lived at approximately the time the main Upanishads are thought to have been composed; his celebrated maxim "everything flows" is very reminiscent of Taoism. But Heraclitus, unfortunately, is known to us only in fragments. Two millennia later, we find what is essentially the Upanishadic theme in the writings of Jan Ruysbroeck, although naturally the terminology is very different. Ruysbroeck puts forward a thoroughly paradoxical view of the nature of God.

> Tranquillity according to His Essence, activity according to His nature: absolute repose, absolute fecundity . . . The Divine Persons who form one sole God are in the fecundity of their nature ever active; and in the simplicity of their essence they form the Godhead. . . . Thus God according to

the Persons is Eternal Work; but according to the Essence and its perpetual stillness, he is Eternal Rest.[12]

How are we to account for these similarities? To me, the only explanation that makes sense is that physical reality and mental reality are, in some way which we find difficult to conceptualize, similar or even identical, and that the laws which govern the subtlest levels of the physical world are the same as those which govern the subtlest levels of the mental world. In this way, whether one explores the nature of matter, the origins of the universe, or the structure of the mind, one is led back and back to a vanishing point of subtlety. What lies beyond?

At this point, language fails. The opening of the *Tao Te Ching* says: "The Tao which can be named is not the eternal Tao." The Vedantists also used negation: Atman (the Self) is *not* this, *not* that. In Buddhism, too, one finds the same failure of language; in the Flower Sermon, the Buddha merely sat silent, holding a flower, and smiled. Much later, a Zen monk described Zen as a finger pointing at the moon. And in Christian mysticism one finds the same note; God, for example, is approached through the "Cloud of Unknowing".

Language *must* be inadequate to describe ultimate Reality, because the moment one uses words one implies differentiation, division; hence one's descriptions can never encompass the Whole. It is, of course, open to the sceptic to say: "All this talk of Tao, Brahman, and so on is mere verbiage; there is nothing beyond the phenomenal world." But what he fails to realize is that the Taoists and Vedantists have cut the ground from under his feet; for to say that this ultimate Reality "exists" is as misleading as to say that it does not exist! Ultimate Reality is logically prior to the world; it is existence itself, pure "Being".

The central difficulty which the materialist faces is to explain why anything should exist at all. This basic question is often lost sight of by philosophers, yet in a way it is the foundation of the whole philosophical enterprise. I once read, in some book on the philosophy of mind which I have now, thankfully, forgotten, the extraordinary statement that the question why anything should exist rather than nothing was an elementary confusion of naive people which could easily be shown up for what it was—although the author did not actually fulfil this interesting undertaking. It is pleasant to know, therefore, that no less prestigious a philosopher than Ludwig Wittgenstein found the question important. In the *Tractatus* (6.44), Wittgenstein wrote: "Not *how* the world is, is the mystical but *that* it is." And Wittgenstein's biographer, Norman Malcolm, records that Wittgenstein

> sometimes had a certain experience which could best be described by saying that "when I have it I *wonder at the existence of the world*. And I am then inclined to use such phrases as 'How extraordinary that anything should exist!' or 'How extraordinary that the world should exist!' ".[13]

Today, the materialists usually have things all their own way; so that we tend too easily to forget that materialism itself is a metaphysical belief.

At the beginning of this chapter, I warned you that we should soon find ourselves in deep water, and now we have done so, for we have fetched up against what has usually been called the realm of Spirit. At this point, preconceptions and difficulties with language come flooding in, and the argument can all too easily become submerged in a welter of confusion. Words such as "Spirit", "God", "Absolute" have been used in so many ways over the last 2,000 years that they have become unmanageable; they carry so many associations and overtones that they convey different things to everyone who uses them.

This, I think, is part of the reason why Maharishi has in recent years moved away from using religious language and instead begun to speak of Creative Intelligence. For people who still cling to the older terms this can cause difficulties, but for the majority, who have rejected conventional religious ideas more or less completely, it is an advantage. One of Maharishi's primary concerns has been to show that the realm of the spiritual is not an area of dreaminess or imprecision, but is on the contrary the supreme reality and can be approached from a scientific angle.

To me, it seems that the new trends in scientific thinking which I have outlined lead in the direction of an exciting new synthesis. The search for the basis of both matter and organization will, I believe, ultimately bring scientists up against that Source which Maharishi calls Creative Intelligence. But that will take a long time, and in any case, even when it happens, it will be merely an intellectual resolution. All the intellect can do is to build up symbolic representations of the world, which bear much the same relation to reality as does the score of a symphony to the sound of the music. What Maharishi, in common with all the great spiritual teachers of earlier times, believes is that true knowledge does not depend on manipulating symbols but is a way of experiencing the world. "Knowledge is structured in consciousness."

Conclusion

If, as begins to appear, the seers who composed ancient texts such as the Upanishads and the *Tao Te Ching* showed such remarkable prescience of the world outlook towards which we seem to be moving, how is this to be explained? How did they get this amazing foreknowledge?

I think that the only answer which makes sense is to suppose that the laws which give rise to the cosmos and those which give rise to our own minds are ultimately the same, and that the ancient notion of a correspondence between man and universe, microcosm and macrocosm, is ultimately correct. The insights of the ancient seers would thus depend on their possessing some means, analogous to TM, for exploring the structure of their minds, and there is in fact good evidence that they did.

Let me make it clear that I am not suggesting that the Vedic or Taoist seers actually anticipated all modern scientific discoveries. My point is rather that their basic outlook on the world, and especially their concept of the way man relates to the rest of Nature, were in the broadest sense organic and ecological, and that this was so because their explorations of their own minds had led them to a profound attunement with the forces that shape the world.

Indeed, unless we do allow for the possibility of such an attunement, we find ourselves faced with a very profound difficulty in the philosophy of science itself; namely, how is it that our minds can provide us with any reliable information about the nature of the world?

This has been a subject of debate among philosophers for centuries. One thing at least seems clear, however; the ability to understand the world is somehow dependent on the structure of our brains. To some people, this has been a source of despair, since they infer that we have no means of being sure that our knowledge has any real validity. According to C. H. Waddington, it was so for Charles Darwin. "Darwin, as the pioneer of evolutionary thinking, was only just escaping from the grip of the old presupposition that knowledge must be totally objective, without any flavour derived from man's own nature . . . "[14]

Total objectivity, Waddington believes, is a myth, and there is no sense in trying to achieve it. But this is not grounds for despair; on the contrary.

> We are a part of nature, and our mind is the only instrument we have, or can conceive of, for learning about nature or ourselves. The idea that during evolution the mentality of animals becomes shaped by its use should no more be a reason for mistrust than is the use-determined curvature of the handle of a scythe or the shape of a knife blade.[15]

We need only take this argument a little further to reach the notion that certain individuals have minds so beautifully shaped by Nature, so finely balanced and adjusted, that they can reflect Reality clearly and directly. This does not mean that they are omniscient, but it does mean that they can discern the underlying pattern of the world; and this is the same at all times.

These are the people the Eastern religions call enlightened. I do not mean to say that it is only in India and China that this form of experience has emerged; on the contrary, it reflects a natural tendency of the human mind, and it is found worldwide. It is, however, in the East that these traditions have reached their greatest degree of perfection, and the current wave of enthusiasm in the West for Eastern philosophies and religions seems to be due to a recognition of this. Maharishi's teachings too, of course, have an Eastern origin, but Maharishi claims that they are not merely Indian but have universal applicability because they are based on the nature of the human mind and hence on cosmic laws.

I pointed out in Chapter One that, at many times in history, it was mystical naturalism and not rationalism which was the ally of science. It seems to me very likely that we are just entering on a period when such co-operation will again be possible and, indeed, essential. And this is the framework in which I would place Maharishi's teaching. Provided our civilization survives, it may eventually produce a synthesis of the scientific and mystical visions which will be at once new and old.

In the next chapter, I want to look at some features of twentieth-century civilization which seem to me to suggest that this synthesis is already beginning to occur.

XIII

Escape from an Impasse

TO SAY THAT we live in a time of profound change is to state
the glaringly obvious. In the last 50 years or so a number of
poets and thinkers have warned us, Cassandra-like, of the coming storm; Nietzsche, W. B. Yeats, and C. G. Jung are names
which come specially to my mind, but there have been many
others. Today there is no more need for warnings; we are in
the midst of the turmoil. Discussions of our troubles fill the
newspapers and take up great quantities of time on television
and radio; diagnoses we have in plenty, but few prescriptions,
and many of those are written by quacks.

Why this seemingly world-wide sense of crisis and doom, of
inability to find solutions to our difficulties? The answer, I
believe, is to be found in the concept of the double bind. We
are, collectively, in a double bind, and are trying to find a
solution at one logical level when it can really be found only
by moving up to the next.

The double bind is a complex one, made up of many elements and operating at many levels. For example, we need
peace if we are to survive yet feel we cannot safely disarm; we
have developed an immensely sophisticated technology without which we cannot maintain our ever-increasing population,
yet which itself seems likely to destroy the environment on
which we depend for our existence; and so on. Probably none
of these problems, singly or collectively, are insoluble. Underlying them all, however, is a deeper difficulty; this is the collective loss of a sense of purpose to which I referred in Chapter One.

The loss of a sense of purpose is itself the outcome of a double
bind. Our brave new world is the creation of our intellects,
and has been achieved largely through the abandonment of
outmoded ways of thinking. And yet it was precisely those
older ways of thinking, which we may broadly call religious,
that gave us a sense of purpose, a place in the scheme of things.
We cannot now turn our backs on the intellect—what we need
today is more intelligence, not less—and yet the intellect

seems to be undermining any remaining sense of belonging we still possess. This, I believe, is the basic double bind we face, and which we must transcend if we are to progress and evolve.

Progress is actually something of a dirty word today. Throughout most of the nineteenth century, it was assumed by almost everyone, more or less as a matter of course, that mankind was progressing. Today we have gone almost wholly to the opposite extreme, and have concluded that the idea of progress is an illusion. If anything, we seem to ourselves to be regressing rather than progressing.

Perhaps the truth lies somewhere between these two extremes. It seems to me that we have encountered a serious evolutionary check; whether it will turn out to be a complete impasse remains to be seen. However, since evolution occurs through the cycle of differentiation and the transcending of double binds, a check presents both a threat and an opportunity.

Throughout most of this book, I have been concerned with the cycle of differentiation as it relates to the individual. The cycle is, I have suggested, the means by which the individual evolves, through the alternate gaining and losing of equilibrium. But this idea does not apply only to individuals; it can also legitimately be applied to the evolution of species, ecologies, and human societies. I believe that the crisis through which we are currently passing is the imbalance phase of a large-scale cycle of differentiation.

There is no need to give detailed instances to show that we are in such an imbalance phase; there is hardly an aspect of our culture which does not confirm the fact. Politics, economics, education, the arts, religion, medicine—all are in confusion, and there seems to be no stability or standards of reference left anywhere.

Since society is a dynamic system, it will respond to imbalance by trying to evolve, to differentiate. That is, it will try to resolve the double bind by some kind of adaptation. At present, such attempts seem to be taking two main forms, orthodox and unorthodox.

By orthodox attempts, I mean those which are primarily political, economic, or technological. Our difficulties are to be overcome by improvements in existing institutions and techniques, or at most by the setting up of new ones—new inventions, and more conferences, agreements, and governmental decrees. Such matters are the concern of those in power. But to an increasingly large number of people, at least in the West, these orthodox solutions seem to be inadequate not merely in practice but also in principle. To people who think in this way, it is our existing habits of thought and behaviour which have brought about our present troubles; how, then, can more thought and behaviour of the same general kind cure those troubles?

This reasoning is surely right. If, as I have suggested, the need is to transcend the double bind in which our society is caught, any effective solution which is found will have to be unorthodox, for orthodox solutions are at the same logical level as the problems and hence are bound to fail. The creative answer to a difficulty must, by definition, consist in a leap to a new level.

Unorthodox solutions are currently being sought in many different areas, but those which are particularly interesting in the present context concern the idea that it is possible to alter human awareness, and that this is the key to resolving our difficulties. It is this belief which underlies two very significant modern trends: the great increase of interest in the paranormal, and the systematic exploration of altered states of awareness. In both cases, many of the people actively involved regard themselves as taking part in a uniquely important endeavour, which, if successful, is destined to change the course of history.

This, of course, is what Maharishi maintains about SCI. So the question naturally arises, what is the relation, if any, between Maharishi's aims and those of people who hold that research into the parnormal or the exploration of altered states of awareness by various means (other than TM) can restore our society to sanity? I want to say something about both activities—the study of the paranormal, and the exploration of "inner space"—and to try to show why, in my opinion, SCI provides the best hope of fulfilling the programme which many of those interested in such matters hope to carry out.

I shall deal with the study of the paranormal and the exploration of altered states of awareness separately, because although there is a good deal of overlapping in practice, in the sense that people who are interested in one are likely to be interested in the other as well, their relevance to Maharishi's ideas is rather different in each case.

The Paranormal

There is today an immense popular interest in the occult, by which I mean a wide range of ideas and practices such as divination, astrology, "fringe" medicine, and unconventional "scientific" theories about Atlantis, UFOs, and so on. Here, however, I am concerned not so much with popular views on the occult as with the increasing acceptance *by scientists* of the idea that the paranormal is not only a valid field of study but has important implications for the future of our society. We have here, I believe, the seeds of a genuine intellectual revolution.

The late Professor C. D. Broad put forward the concept of what he called "basic limiting principles". These are the presuppositions which, he said, are accepted by almost everyone who has been brought up within or under the influence of a modern technological society and which guide our thinking about what is and is not conceivable. Broad compiled a list of these principles, although he did not claim that it was comprehensive; indeed, one of the most characteristic features of the basic limiting principles is that they are tacit and not easy to recognize.

For example, a biologist who writes a textbook on evolution does not normally start by denying the doctrine of special creation; he assumes, as a matter of course, that none of his readers believe in this, and he is likely to be right. When Darwin wrote *The Origin of Species* that was not the case; in those days the basic limiting principles were different.

Again—and this is more directly relevant to my theme—another basic limiting principle is that it is impossible to obtain information, from another person's mind or from anywhere else, except, directly or indirectly, through sensory means. This rules out telepathy and clairvoyance. Similar basic limiting principles can be defined to exclude precognition and psychokinesis (the moving of objects by paranormal means).

Now, what seems to be happening today is that certain of the basic limiting principles are being called more and more into question. Among non-scientists they were never, perhaps, taken as seriously as many rationalists supposed, but today many people have ceased to pay them the lip-service which they did in the past. And this is not true only of lay people; a number of scientists are also coming to question the basic limiting principles. Papers on the paranormal appear in even the most orthodox establishment scientific journals, such as *Nature*, and well-known scientists are not ashamed to admit that they take an interest in such matters.

The acceptance of the paranormal by scientists seems, to the more orthodox-minded, a real *trahison des clercs*. To such critics, we seem to be entering on a new Dark Age of superstition; before long, probably, we shall see the appointment of an Astrologer Royal, and heads of government will begin each day by peering into the entrails of sacrificial chickens.

Such fears are exaggerated, no doubt, but there is today a real shift in attitudes towards the paranormal, and not only among the unsophisticated.

The reason why many rationalists object to the scientific study of the paranormal is that they fear it may open the back door of the citadel of reason to religion. And certainly this idea (as a hope rather than as a fear) was in the minds of many of the founders of the Society for Psychical Research (of which, incidentally, Broad was both a member and a past President). The aims of the society, which was founded by Henry Sidgwick and a group of fellow Cambridge intellectuals in 1882, were "to examine without prejudice or prepossession and in a scientific spirit those faculties of man, real or supposed, which appear to be inexplicable to any generally recognized hypothesis". The society, it should be noted, did not (and does not) hold or express any corporate views.

By the closing years of the nineteenth century it was already becoming obvious to many intelligent people—and Sidgwick and his colleagues were among the ablest of their time—that scientific materialism had fatally undermined conventional Christianity, especially as regards the belief in an afterlife. Seeing clearly the dangerous implications of such undermining for the stability of society, and feeling keenly within themselves the vacuum left by the collapse of these comforting beliefs, Sidgwick and his group devoted a vast amount of money, time, and effort to the task of trying to obtain scientific evidence on the subject. In the end, many of them believed that they had succeeded.

How much they really achieved is ultimately a matter of opinion. All that can safely be said is that no one who has not examined at least a part of the immensely complicated accumulated material (to examine it *all* would be a lifetime's work in itself) is in a position to make a valid judgement. What is certain, however, is that enough evidence has accumulated over the years, from the work of the society and other sources, to make it clear that there is a great deal more to the human mind than the positivists suppose. Alan Gauld concludes his fascinating book *The Founders of the Society For Psychical Research* as follows:

> The results which the Sidgwick group obtained in its twenty years of earnest labours may at any rate be used to hammer that over-zealous brand of "mechanical rationalism" which hopes by exhibiting "personality" as the blind output of physical forces to leave in an ordered Universe not one single Gothic protuberance on which religion can scrape a toehold. Against this obsessive tidy-mindedness it is possible to launch a modest arsenal of spiky facts; facts which strongly suggests that not all manifestations of personality can be understood within the accepted framework of biological science. Any rationalist who studies and thinks about these facts, dispassionately and in detail will, I should guess, find himself in deep and unsuspected waters from which no shore is clearly visible, and least of all to him.[1]

This seems to me a very fair summing-up of the position. What is happening today, however, is that serious researchers into the paranormal have found themselves overtaken by events, and some of them are not quite sure what to make of the new state of affairs. For many years, the student of such matters was looked on as a crank by most scientists and laymen alike. Today the scientific community as a whole persists in this attitude, though as I have said the rock is beginning to crumble; but the attitude of the lay public is changing rapidly and dramatically. This change, however, is not due to any startling discoveries by researchers into the paranormal; rather it is due to a shift in the way people think, which has brought to the surface a will to believe. More than ever before in modern times, people in general are looking for wonders. Serious researchers cannot supply them at the required rate, so less serious researchers are filling the gap and purveying wonders.

The present situation with regard to the paranormal is a little like that which prevailed in relation to exotic countries in the Renaissance. Then, as now, people were bursting intellectual bonds and looking abroad for wonders, which unscrupulous travel writers were not slow to supply. Hence readers were fed tales of men whose heads grew beneath their shoulders in the middle of their chests, who had only one leg, or whose ears were so large that they could wrap them right round their bodies. Today there are hardly any unexplored areas left on earth, but the world of the mind is still almost unknown. And here be dragons.

The public, in short, gets what it wants. But that does not mean that there are *no* wonders to be described in the world of the mind, any more than the mendaciousness of many early travellers meant that everywhere else was really just like home. On the contrary, modern zoology and anthropology has revealed a far richer and more interesting world than any fantasist ever imagined. So, too, with the mind; there is far more to human nature than the rationalists of the nineteenth century were willing to allow.[2]

The real question, it seems to me, is not *whether* paranormal phenomena occur—they do—but what they mean. Having established their existence, where do we go from there?

Not long ago I received a letter asking if I would agree to the inclusion of my name as a member of a network of scientists interested in the paranormal. The aim of the organization was to circulate information of interest to members and to provide a subterranean pressure group which could help to bring home to the scientific community at large the importance of psychical research. Although I agreed to add my name, since I was broadly in sympathy with the aims of the organization, I did so without any real expectation that such a group could have much effect. At one time I used to believe that psychical research (or parapsychology, as it has recently been rechristened in America) would help to restore a more "spiritual" view of man, but I no longer think that it is likely to have much effect of that kind. I have in fact come to believe that the practical importance of this kind of research is much less than many enthusiasts suppose.

Those who regard psychical research as potentially of great importance reason something like this. The trouble with modern life is that it is too materialistic. If we can prove that there is more to human nature than the rationalists allow—if the basic limiting principles can be shown not to hold—then this information will, provided it is presented sufficiently cogently, bring about a reversion to a less materialistic world outlook.

This argument looks good at first glance, but I do not think it will stand up to serious examination. Let us suppose, for the sake of argument, that incontrovertible evidence of the reality of paranormal phenomena such as telepathy, clairvoyance, and precognition were obtained, such that no reasonable person could gainsay it. What would follow?

We would be presented with a set of facts which were inexplicable within the present conceptual framework, and this would present a great challenge to our best minds. Presumably in the end some new conceptual framework would be established to accommodate the new facts—the boundaries would be redrawn—but I do not think that any profound ethical reappraisal would necessarily follow. There do not, in fact, seem to be any particular connections between what people believe and how they behave; some of the greatest crimes in history have been commited by religious believers and indeed have sometimes been perpetrated in the name of religion, while some exemplary individuals have been agnostics or atheists.

It might be, then, that the new evidence would make no real difference at all. There is, however, another possibility, namely, that the effects would be actively harmful. This idea needs to be looked at in a little more detail.

Throughout history, nearly all the great spiritual masters have cautioned their pupils against becoming diverted by the pursuit of paranormal phenomena. The various techniques for gaining enlightenment which developed in India and China, and to a lesser extent in the West, apparently tend to produce various paranormal phenomena as an incidental effect, and the literature of the mystically-orientated religions contains many warnings against losing one's way in these attractive side-channels.

For example, there seems to be little doubt that there exist techniques for inducing "out-of-the-body experiences" (astral travelling). Whether one regards such experiences as hallucinatory or in some sense real is not important; what matters is that they do occur spontaneously (probably much more frequently than is generally realized, since many people in our society would hesitate to mention them for fear of being thought mad), and there seems to be no good reason why some people at least should not be able to induce them deliberately.

In fact, a number of Westerners have claimed to be able to do precisely this, and have published descriptions of the methods they used. The most recent example is Robert A. Monroe, who has described his own experiences in a recent book, *Journeys out of the Body*. As the history of LSD makes plain, if a reliable and reasonably easy technique for inducing such experiences exists and becomes widely known, a great many people will take advantage of it. Is this desirable?

Even if the experiences are wholly hallucinatory—merely exceptionally vivid dreams—it might not be wise to indulge in them. True, Mr Monroe claims to have suffered no ill effects from repeated "trips", but some of his experiences sound alarming enough and would undoubtedly be dangerously disturbing to anyone whose mental balance was less than ideal.

But, as Monroe very pertinently remarks, what if the experiences are *not* hallucinatory? What if it were possible to eavesdrop on secret meetings, or even to injure or kill someone when one was "out of the body"? (Monroe claims that on one such trip he inflicted a bruise on a distant friend by pinching her.) These notions, I fully admit, are almost certainly the veriest moonshine, but that is not the point. What I want to emphasize is that the effects of convincing people in general of the reality of paranormal phenomena might not be at all what is hoped, even—or perhaps especially—if the phenomena in question *are* real. When one contemplates what humanity has done so far with the knowledge it has gained about the physical world, one cannot be very sanguine about the effects of injecting a vast amount of information about the realm of the paranormal.*

The equation, which many people seem to accept unthinkingly, between the paranormal and the spiritual seems to me a

---

* In recent years there have been persistent rumours that the military on both sides of the Iron Curtain have been taking an interest in ESP and allied matters. If this is true, it would hardly be a matter for surprise.

most dubious one. In her celebrated book *Mysticism*, Evelyn Underhill drew an important distinction between the mystic and the magician. The magician attempts to gain power for his own sake, whereas the mystic wants to become a channel for spiritual forces to express themselves. Although there is certainly a good deal of overlapping between the two approaches, the difference is none the less clear enough in most cases for there to be no question about its reality; one has only to set St John of the Cross against Aleister Crowley ("The Beast") to see what is meant.

Contrary to what many people believe, I do not think that even a conclusive demonstration of post-mortem survival would have the beneficial results which some advocates of psychical research suppose. We are sometimes told that if we believed in a future life, whether on this earth or elsewhere, we would behave better in the present one. The comparative failure of campaigns to stop people smoking—a habit whose ill effects are produced in this life, not the next—does not encourage much optimism about the efficacy of appeals based on future happiness.

At the same time, I do not want to go to the opposite extreme and deny that psychical research has any practical importance at all. Its value, I think, is just what Alan Gauld expressed in the passage I have already quoted; it gives a sense of possibilities and enlarges one's mental horizons. In this respect, it is strictly comparable to any of the other natural sciences, such as physics, biology, or psychology. It tells us something new about the world by pushing back the boundary of knowledge, but the new knowledge which it supplies is ethically neutral. When we have made our parapsychological discoveries, we shall still be just where we were so far as our moral and spiritual advancement is concerned; everything will still be to do.

In my own case, I have derived a good deal of intellectual help from the findings of psychical research, and, as I shall point out in the next chapter, I think that these findings can shed light on certain important historical events. But the importance of psychical research remains limited, I am sure, and the distinction between the mystic and the magician is one which should always be kept in mind.

The Exploration of Inner Space

We come now to the second kind of unorthodox approach to the problems of our time. In the last few years the vivid expression "inner space" has been applied to the mind, the suggestion being that the inner world offers a field of exploration as vast and potentially as important as that of interstellar space. (Notice, incidentally, the implied reference to the microcosm-macrocosm equation.) Notions of this kind have been current among some younger American psychologists for a number of years now. In 1961 the American Association for Humanistic Psychology was founded under the inspiration of Abraham Maslow, Carl Rogers, Gardner Murphy (a psychologist with a long-standing interest in parapsychology) and others, and in 1969 an influential anthology of readings edited by Charles Tart, a psychologist and parapsychologist at the University of California, appeared under the title *Altered States of Consciousness*. All this activity was evidence of a profound sense of dissatisfaction with the narrow limits imposed by the behaviourist orthodoxy in which these researchers had been brought up. In 1969, too, there appeared the first issue of the *Journal of Transpersonal Psychology* (with which Maslow, again, was associated until his recent death). This publication contains a "Statement of Purpose" which says that it is concerned with

> ... meta-needs, ultimate values, unitive consciousness, peak experiences, ecstasy, mystical experience ... essence, bliss, awe, wonder, self-actualization, ultimate meaning, transcendence of the self, spirit, sacralization of every-day life, oneness, cosmic awareness, cosmic play, individual and species-wide synergy, transcendental phenomena. ...*

As this outline will show, many of the inner space explorers have been scientists or academics, but their attitude to their material is frequently not that of academics. Instead of maintaining a discreet distance from the phenomena they are studying, they become involved at first hand, and although their

* One issue contains an interesting article by Tart on his first year's experience with TM; see "A Psychologist's experience with Transcendental Meditation", *Journal of Transpersonal Psychology*, 1971, Vol. 2, p. 135.

writings preserve the trappings (and, unfortunately, sometimes the jargon) of professional academic articles, their content
often verges on the religious or mystical. Moreover, underlying much of the literature of the new psychology is the idea
that the importance of their discoveries range far beyond the
merely academic. Here, for example, are the words of one
scientific heretic, John C. Lilly. Lilly has a medical degree
and trained as a psychoanalyst; he has worked as a researcher
in electronics, biophysics, neurology and neuroanatomy; in
particular, he has studied the mind of the dolphin. In the last
few years, however, he has left orthodox science to explore,
personally, various altered states of consciousness. In the
Introduction to his book describing his experiences, *The
Centre of the Cyclone*, he writes as follows:

> In this book I speak as one who has been to the highest
> state of consciousness [sic] or of Satori-Samadhi, and as
> one who has returned to report to those interested . . .
>   It is my firm belief that the experience of higher states of
> consciousness is necessary for survival of the human species.
> If we can each experience at least the lower level of Satori,
> there is hope that we won't blow up the planet or otherwise
> eliminate life as we know it. If every person on the planet,
> especially those in power in the establishments, can even-
> tually reach high levels or states regularly, the planet will
> be run with relatively simple efficiency and joy. Problems
> such as pollution, slaughter of other species, over-production,
> famine, disease, and war will then be solved by the rational
> application of realizable means.[3]

One may have reservations about some of the claims made
by Lilly and his fellow explorers, but it is surely both exciting
and important that Western intellectuals should be writing in
this way; it points to that attempt to find radically new solutions to our problems which, I have suggested, is the only
chance we have for evolving.
People like Lilly have seen where the solution to our difficulties lies. And yet it must be admitted that the wheat is
mixed with a great deal of chaff; some good books and articles
have appeared, and also a great deal that is worthless. This
makes it difficult for the outsider to assess the scene as a whole;

even if he is sympathetic to the inner space idea, and agrees
with Lilly and others that the answer to our problem must be
sought within, he may well feel that, on the practical level,
he is confronted by an embarrassment of riches: too many
kinds of meditation, too many "paths to enlightenment".
How is he to choose among them? A lifetime would not be
long enough to sample more than a few; and even if there were
more time, what standards of comparison should be used?

Anyone who intends to explore inner space requires two
things: a vehicle and a map. As to the vehicle, it seemed at one
time (to many people, at least) that LSD and the other psychedelic drugs would be ideal. Impetus was given to this idea in
the late 1950s by Aldous Huxley's book *The Doors of Perception*;
modern prophets such as Timothy Leary soon arose to preach
the gospel of LSD with a good deal of eloquence, and the
vogue for drug-induced mysticism was under way.

A large amount of literature about the effects of drugs has
now accumulated. From this it is evident that these effects
are remarkably variable, but in some cases the descriptions
are closely similar to those given by people who have had
natural mystical experience. A number of drug takers, starting
with Aldous Huxley, have not hesitated to claim that the two
sorts of experience are, in fact, identical.* So striking can the
effects sometimes be that many people, not all of them foolish
or gullible, have believed that we now have a chemical path-
way to the furthest reaches of religious mysticism. If one accepts
this, however, one has also to accept that mystical experience
is in some sense abnormal;† that is, it is a temporary vision
which may perhaps provide insights of supreme importance

* The fact that people describe their experiences in the same
terms does not, of course, prove that the experiences are the same
or even very similar, especially in the case of mystical and allied
experience, which is notoriously difficult to put into words.

† Although the action of the hallucinogens such as LSD and
mescalin is not fully understood, it seems probable that they are
artificial neurotransmitters. That is, the molecules of which they
are made is similar in shape to those of naturally occurring substances in the brain which normally trigger nerve cells by passing
across the tiny gap which separates them. In this way, the drugs
are thought to block the receptor sites on the cells, "jamming"
them like keys which almost fit a lock but not quite.

but which is not desirable as a permanent state. But, for the great mystics of both East and West, the goal is not a temporary insight, however valuable, but a *permanent* transformation of awareness. It does not seem likely that any drug we shall discover in the foreseeable future will produce that kind of change.

Partly, perhaps, because of disillusion with the effects of drugs, and partly also because the use of LSD and similar drugs was made illegal in many countries during the 1960s, many researchers have moved towards non-pharmacological methods of inducing unusual experiences. These have included hypnosis, listening to repeating words on tape, sensory deprivation, various forms of meditation, and, more recently, biofeedback. Such techniques have proved as effective as drugs for leading to inner space and are—presumably—less dangerous.

But what have the experiences so induced to do with enlightenment? Here we touch on what, to my mind, is the great weakness of much of the inner space literature. Most of it places far too much emphasis on experiences, the underlying assumption being that the more strange and dramatic an experience is, the greater its value. The purpose of many of the inner space explorers seems to be to induce various forms of transcendental experience and then to reflect on them afterwards, endeavouring to integrate the insights so obtained into the rest of life.

Maharishi's approach is quite different and—in my view—much more profound. He is not concerned with experiences during meditation except in so far as they indicate refinement of the nervous system *which has already occurred*. This is an essential principle of his teaching. For him, meditation is a physiological process before it is a psychological one, and its purpose is to release stress. Once stress has been released a dramatic experience may sometimes follow, but this is relatively unimportant. What really matters is the physiological change. Enlightenment, Maharishi insists, is not anything strange but is simply the state of full physiological and psychological normality.

This is not wholly to deny the possibility that valuable experiences may, on occasion, be associated with the use of psychedelic drugs and various techniques for inducing abnormal brain states, but it seems to be generally accepted, even by those who have used drugs, that these substances do not produce the experiences but only release what is already potentially present. That is, people who take drugs experience what it is in them to experience.

The purpose of TM is quite different. It is to *allow* (not force) the brain to refine its structure and organization naturally, so that the capacity for experience and action is enhanced. For this to occur, there has to be a continual oscillation between meditation and activity, in the manner which I have described. Maharishi therefore emphasizes the rôle of activity in the growth towards enlightenment, and he also emphasizes that the purpose of practising TM is to enrich everyday life. In other words, although TM is a vehicle for the exploration of inner space, that exploration is set firmly in the context of *outer* space—of the real world, in which we live and act.

It is this emphasis on activity which makes Maharishi's teaching of such vital practical importance today. Those inner space explorers who, like Lilly, believe that the way to restore collective sanity to the world is through inner experience are right, but it is one thing to recognize this in principle and quite another to translate it into practice as Maharishi has done. Maharishi's aims are astonishingly ambitious; the scope of his vision is enormous. He speaks openly of regenerating mankind and of transforming society. In my final chapter, I want to look at the ideas which underlie this bold programme, and to try to relate them to the concept of the cycle of differentiation as it applies to society.

XIV

Freedom and Necessity

IN THE LAST chapter, I suggested that the search for new forms of awareness which has been so characteristic a feature of the second half of the twentieth century can best be seen as an attempt by our society to evolve by transcending the double bind in which it finds itself. This idea has further implications which I should like to bring out.

There are two approaches one might use to try to understand what is going on in the world today. One is to adopt the tools and concepts of the conventional historian, and to look for social forces, economic factors, and the rest. This approach has its place, and I certainly do not want to decry its importance. There is, however, another approach, which you will not find in the history books but which nevertheless seems to me to be a necessary complement to the first.

I think I can best illustrate my meaning by referring to a curious historical phenomenon for which there seems to be no adequate explanation in conventional terms; this is the near-simultaneity with which certain great ethical, religious, and philosophical ideas have appeared in the world. Thus, Confucius is thought to have been born about 550 BC, the Buddha about 560; Mahavira (the founder of Jainism) was also born about 560, and Zoroaster (if a historical personage) about 600. This vintage period for religious teachers also probably saw the composition of the great Upanishads. Heraclitus, whose philosophy, from the little we know of it, resembled that of his great Eastern near-contemporaries in important respects, was teaching in Greece in about 500 BC.

It is not only religious ideas which show this mysterious simultaneity; the same is true of quite mundane matters, such as technology and science. Joseph Needham remarks that the influence of the phases of the moon on the reproduction of shellfish was recognized in both Europe and China in the fourth century AD; he also points out that various inventions, such as toothed wheels, the waterwheel, and the camera obscura were made almost simultaneously in both parts of the world although no direct influence has been traced (this does not mean, of course, that it did not exist). Even more surprising, perhaps, is the fact that the study of anatomy arose *and declined* at much the same period in both Europe and China. Needham comments: "The simultaneities are sometimes troubling. Some ideas, some sciences, and some complicated inventions have a disagreeable habit of appearing (and even disappearing) almost at the same time at both ends of the Old World."[1]

Coincidences such as these are undoubtedly "quite troubling" to anyone who insists on taking a rigidly materialistic view of human life and awareness. However—and this, perhaps, is the area where research into the paranormal has its greatest practical relevance—they need not be puzzling if one is willing to revise one's basic limiting principles.

One scientist who was very willing to do this, and to incorporate the paranormal into his theories, was C. G. Jung. In his concept of the "collective unconscious" Jung provided a framework for thinking about simultaneities of the kind I am considering. This is not the place to discuss Jung's ideas, but let me simplify them to the point of caricature and say that Jung favoured an "island" theory of human personality. Each individual is like an island projecting above the surface of the sea, separate from all the others above the water line but joined with them below. At a superficial level, minds (and thoughts) are individual, but at a deeper level they are one.

Jung's psychology is by no means universally accepted, it is true, and many people would not allow that it is scientific. I do not myself find it by any means wholly satisfactory, yet I believe that Jung saw further into the depths of the mind than probably any other recent Western thinker. He certainly held that profound shifts in the balance of human awareness had occurred in the past—for example, at the beginning of the Christian era—and that a shift of comparable importance was taking place now; and in his concept of the collective unconscious he formulated principles which go at least part of the way towards describing the forces that produce such shifts.

Although Jung did not, so far as I know, ever use cybernetic terms, the concepts of cybernetics and of "General Systems Theory" seem to me to have a good deal of applicability to his ideas, for he thought of the psyche—individual and collective—as a dynamic system, in which interchange was constantly going on between conscious and unconscious levels.

The Jungian view of the psyche could, I think, be described as an ecological one, in the sense that the psyche is the resultant of an interplay of many factors seeking to come to balance. And to me it suggests that the near-simultaneous appearance of similar ideas throughout the world at certain times is not due to cultural contacts alone, but is also the outcome of changes occurring within the ecological system of the collective unconscious.

Now, I do not want to seem to put words into Maharishi's mouth, but I think that his view of the historical process as he sets it out in his *Commentary* on the *Bhagavad Gita* is compatible, to put it no higher, with the theory I have put forward. It may seem a bit far-fetched to read the ideas of "General Systems Theory" into a religious classic such as the *Gita*, and yet although the language is naturally very different the underlying concepts, I believe, are not.

Here is Krishna, the Lord of Creation, describing to Arjuna the process by which harmony is restored in Nature.

> Whenever dharma is in decay and adharma flourishes, O Bharata [Arjuna], then I create myself.
>
> To protect the righteous and destroy the wicked, to establish dharma firmly, I take birth age after age.[2]

Dharma is a difficult word to translate. Maharishi says that it refers to:

> specific modes of activity or different ways of righteousness, which keep the whole stream of life in harmony—every aspect of life being *properly balanced* [my italics] with every other aspect—and moving in the direction of evolution. . . . "Adharma" means absence of dharma. When adharma prevails, the great power of nature, which maintains the equilibrium between positive and negative forces, is lost, and the process of evolution is thereby obstructed.[3]

Thus it is *loss of balance* which, according to Maharishi's interpretation of the *Gita*, brings about a counter-force designed to
restore order.

> The equilibrium of the three gunas [that is, the basic forces
> of nature which are supposed to underlie all creation and to
> produce the phenomenal world by their interplay] is main-
> tained automatically, just as law and order are automatically
> maintained by a government. But whenever a crisis arises,
> the head of state has to exercise his special power. When-
> ever dharma is in decay, the balance of the three gunas is
> disturbed, the equilibrium in nature is lost, the path of
> evolution is distorted and chaos prevails.[4]

This is surely a perfect statement of the principle of homeostasis. Whenever balance begins to be lost, the cycle of differentiation tends to come into play to restore it; and the
outcome is evolution.

At present we are in just such a situation of imbalance,
adharma, and that is why the knowledge of how to contact one's
inner depths through TM has reappeared. Our time is not
unique in this respect; the knowledge has been found and lost
and found again many times in the past. Why does it become
lost?

> The reason for its loss . . . is "the long lapse of time" . . .
> While its principle is imperishable its practice needs periodic
> revival, according to the changed conditions of living from
> age to age. Because it awakens man's consciousness to
> extreme purity, this system of Yoga is equally suitable for
> people in every age. Sometimes, however, it is not followed
> in its pure form; then the desired results are not achieved
> and this eventually leads to indifference towards its practice.
> Thus this great principle of life becomes lost from time to
> time. But it cannot be lost for ever, because, as the Truth
> of existence, it must be brought to light again and again.
> Nature helps to restore it. From time to time great teachers
> come with the proper inspiration to reveal the path once
> more. They renew the tradition which maintains the teach-
> ing. The renewed tradition remains dominant so long as it
> continues to inspire the people. But when it fails to respond

to the need of the age new teachers arise. This cycle is repeated again and again.[5]

From these passages, it will be clear that Maharishi thinks of the process whereby spiritual values flow into the world as essentially naturalistic. This is a typically Eastern view. In the West, we have—until recently at any rate—believed in a personal God who promulgates edicts to us; the analogy which comes to mind is that of a lawgiver governing his subjects by decree.

This way of thinking had a far-reaching effect on the way science developed in the West. To the thinkers of the eighteenth and nineteenth centuries, it was natural to picture the universe as a giant mechanism, which had been constructed and set going by the Great Artificer. And when the notion of a personal Deity finally disappeared from science altogether, all that was left was a soulless mechanism operating according to impersonal laws.

We have here a counterpart on the grand scale to the mind-body problem. The body, like the universe, is a mechanism. So long as people believed in a ruling soul—a ghost to operate the mechanism—all was more or less well, but when that idea ceased to be credible all that was left was the mechanism; and what then became of the will? What caused our actions?

All these difficulties were avoided by most of the major schools of Eastern philosophy, which lacked the concept of a Lawgiver and hence were not obliged to encounter the consequences of his demise. This has been brought out with special clarity for China (by Needham), but the Indian concept of the universe seems to have been broadly similar. In both cases, the universe was regarded, not as being composed of dead matter wholly separate from mind, but as an organic unity, in which human life was one strand in an over-all pattern.

It may well be, as Needham implies, that modern science would not have developed without the Western picture of a mechanical cosmos presided over by a Lawgiver. But we are now at the point where we are being forced, by the logic of our own scientific dicoveries, towards a more "organismic" view of nature—a view which has much in common with that of the ancient Far East.

Certainly it is an organismic view of this kind which seems

to be implied by Maharishi's references to the "Laws of Nature". For Maharishi, the universe is by no means soulless or dead. On the contrary, our human values emerge from, and find their justification in, the structure of the cosmos.

Some people may find this idea satisfying, as I do myself; others at first may not. For, to many moderns, the whole point of being human is precisely that one is *not* at the complete mercy of the "blind, impersonal forces of the universe". However puny one's voice may be, one can at least stand up for a brief instant and shout one's defiance in the teeth of the gale. This existentialist view of man sets great store by "human freedom" and anyone who subscribes to it is likely to find Maharishi's thesis unacceptable.

My own view is that the central thesis of existentialism is based on a mistaken notion of human freedom. Clearly this is a vast subject, and to do it anything like justice would require a book to itself. Nevertheless, it is so important that I want to spend a little time looking at it in the context of Maharishi's description of enlightenment.

Freedom and Necessity

The difference between the mechanical and the organic conceptions of Nature are well brought out in some lines of William Blake:

cruel Works
Of many wheels I view, wheel without wheel, with cogs tyrannic
Moving by compulsion each other, not as those in Eden, which,
Wheel within wheel, in freedom revolve in harmony and in peace.[6]

According to the true understanding of causality—that which obtains in "Eden"—freedom and necessity are not alternatives but are complementary, like light and shade, good and evil, male and female, Yin and Yang. You cannot have one without the other (although the duality can be transcended on the level of experience, in the state which Maharishi calls Unity-consciousness).

Perhaps that sounds over-metaphysical, so let me try to put it in more concrete terms.

Consider artistic creation. People often hanker after creativity because they feel that it must be associated with freedom, and so in a way it is. But, paradoxically, it is also associated with necessity. Not long ago I heard a perceptive music critic, discussing Beethoven's life, say that at the end of his career the composer had reached a state of "absolute freedom, absolute necessity". And this, I am sure, is right. It has often been remarked that the characteristic feature of great art is that it combines complete freedom with complete inevitability. A really well-made poem, or novel, or painting, or piece of music feels right; it could not have been otherwise. It expresses the impulse to creativity—to spontaneity—at its fullest, and yet it is wholly determined by its inner necessity.

That this should be so is perhaps obvious when one thinks about the matter. Take the case of writing. To the insensitive writer, one word or phrase is as good as another; as a result, his meaning, if it comes across at all, does so foggily and imprecisely. The good writer, on the other hand, has many more constraints on his choice of words and construction of sentences. He has to take into account not only the exact meaning he wishes to convey and the best words to convey this meaning, he has also to get the balance of his sentences right by ear, almost like a musician tuning an instrument or a craftsman shaping the handle of a tool.

Failure to recognize all the constraints operating on language can lead to sentences like: "The eminent statistician rubbed his ear thoughtfully and produced a cigarette." Or: "Bob guided her to the spinet. He took his spectacles off his beaky nose and invited Mrs Ransome to admire it. 'It's much smaller than Aunt Bertha's,' she said." (Both appeared in short stories.)

In one sense the careless or insensitive writer is freer than the careful and sensitive one—free to choose his words carelessly—but in another, more important, sense he is not free at all, for he is unable to communicate effectively. The principle is taken to its extreme by poetry, where the number of constraints operating is (or should be) much greater than in the case of prose.

We find exactly the same principle at work in science.

Needham quotes Francis Bacon as saying, "We cannot command Nature except by obeying her." And there are the well-known words of Thomas Henry Huxley, written in a letter to Charles Kingsley on the occasion of the death of Huxley's son, aged four.

> Science seems to me to teach in the highest and strongest manner the great truth which is embodied in the Christian conception of entire surrender to the will of God. Sit down before fact as a little child, be prepared to give up every preconceived notion, follow humbly wherever and to whatever abysses Nature leads, or you shall learn nothing.[7]

The second sentence of that passage is often quoted, but usually without the first. Yet how fascinating it is that Huxley, whom one usually thinks of as the first apostle of nineteenth-century rationalism, should have linked the scientific and religious attitudes in this way. As Needham points out, any Taoist philosopher could have written that passage; and so too, I think, could Maharishi. For at the core of his teaching we find this idea—that freedom and necessity are ultimately the same, and that the only true freedom consists in acting in accordance with the laws of Nature.

In reality, *all* our actions are the results of the working out of cosmic forces. To this extent, the determinists are right. But determinism becomes true only if one takes *all* the cosmic forces into account, and at this universal level the distinction between free will and determinism ceases to have any meaning.

Enlightenment—"liberation"—consists in the realization *on the level of experience* of this truth about the nature of causation. The enlightened individual perceives that all activity proceeds in accordance with natural forces. The *Gita* puts this view forward in several verses.

> One who is in Union with the Divine and who knows the Truth will maintain "I do not act at all".[8]

> Actions are in every case performed by the three gunas of Nature. He whose mind is deluded by the sense of "I" holds "I am the doer".
> But he who knows the truth about the divisions of the gunas

and their actions ... knowing that it is the gunas which act upon the gunas, remains unattached.[9]

Maharishi's comment on this teaching is as follows:

The authorship of action does not in reality belong to the "I". It is a mistake to understand that "I" do this, "I" experience this and "I" know this. All this is basically untrue. The "I", in its essential nature, is uncreated; it belongs to the field of the Absolute. Whereas action, its fruits and the relationship between the doer and his action belong to the relative field, to the field of the three gunas. Therefore all action is performed by the three gunas born of Nature. The attribution of authorship to the "I" is only due to ignorance of the real nature of the "I" and of action.[10]

According to Maharishi, then, enlightenment consists in recognizing that we do not really act, but merely witness the forces of nature working themselves out.

This is a very subtle idea, which can easily be misunderstood. I must emphasize, therefore, that it does *not* mean that action in the real world is unimportant or irrelevant. On the contrary, solutions to the complex technological, political, and social problems we face can be found only through hard thinking and effective action. Enlightenment is not merely compatible with activity, it presupposes it, as Maharishi is at pains to make clear.

The intellect of the man who is not realized is wholly involved with activity. The realized should not create a division in such a man's mind. He should not talk to him of the separateness of the Self from activity, otherwise the ignorant man may lose interest in practical life, and if this happens he will never be able to gain realization. It is not the intellectual understanding of the separateness of the Divine and of activity, but rather the experience of this state which brings a man enlightenment.[11]

According to Needham, exactly the same teaching about the nature of action is to be found in Taoism, and exactly the same misunderstanding has occurred on the part of later commentators. One of the most characteristic of Taoist ideals was *wu wei*, which is usually translated as "non-action". According to Needham, however, this is a mistake, and the real meaning of the term is "action in accordance with the laws of Nature". Thus, in the *Huai Nan Tzu* we read:

> Some may maintain that the person who acts in the spirit of *wu wei* is one who is serene and does not speak, or one who meditates and does not move; he will not come when called nor be driven by force. And this demeanour, it is assumed, is the appearance of one who has obtained the Tao. Such an interpretation of *wu wei* I cannot admit. I never heard such an explanation from any sage.[12]

And you will not hear such an interpretation from Maharishi either. In the *Gita* Arjuna asks Krishna: "What are the signs of a man whose intellect is steady, who is absorbed in the Self, O Keshava? How does the man of steady intellect speak, how does he sit, how does he walk?"[13]

To this, Krishna replies: "When a man completely casts off all desires that have gone [deep] into the mind, O Partha, when he is satisfied in the Self through the Self alone, then he is said to be of steady intellect."[14]

In other words, as Maharishi points out in his *Commentary*, enlightenment does not produce any special signs or behaviour. "The inner state of such a man cannot be judged by outer signs. It cannot be said that he sits like this or looks like that or closes his eyes in any particular manner. No such external signs can serve as criteria of this state."[15]

What seems to have happened in both India and China is that the original teaching about action in accordance with Nature became misunderstood as doing nothing at all. The point is subtle, but vitally important. The enlightened should never "make a mood" of non-attachment or inaction; rather, through the practice of TM, actions should be allowed to become spontaneously more in tune with Creative Intelligence. But action always continues. Thus Krishna (who, it will be remembered, is here speaking as the Lord of the universe) says:

> What if I did not continue unwearyingly in activity, O Partha [Arjuna]? Men in every way follow my example.

If I did not engage in action, these worlds would perish and I would be the cause of confusion and of the destruction of these people.[16]

Thus, activity is part of the very nature of existence, and cannot cease even for an instant. To suppose otherwise is to fall into a fundamentally mistaken notion of the way the universe is constituted. And yet it remains true that "all action is performed by the three gunas born of Nature", and that the "I" does not really act at all. Evidently we have come up against a basic paradox, which cannot be resolved intellectually.

On the conceptual level, to say that we are free although our actions are determined by the ebb and flow of cosmic forces is a contradiction; if we try to understand this intellectually, we inevitably take hold of one horn of the dilemma to the exclusion of the other, and the natural result is either complete irresponsibility or complete submission to "fate". It is vital to understand that the true state of liberation, although it can be described, cannot be imagined; it can only be lived. For most of us, the nearest we come to it is at moments of artistic or intellectual creation, when everything is seen to be both right and inevitable. Bateson quotes J. S. Bach as saying of his method of composition: "I play the notes in order, as they are written. It is God who makes the music." The state of liberation, it appears, is one in which we perform our actions in order, as they are written.

It is in this light that we should understand the changes in the collective unconscious which are occurring today.

I believe that we are currently experiencing the beginnings of an inflow of a great current of Creative Intelligence, order, pattern—call it what you will—and that our one hope of survival lies in taking advantage of that current. No doubt the main flood has broken up into many smaller streams and rivulets, each of which has its own value, but in my view Maharishi's teaching represents the main thrust and so offers us the best chance of restoring our collective sanity.

For society to be transformed, Maharishi holds, there is no need for all, or even a majority, of society to practise TM; as few as one in a hundred would suffice. Maharishi compares society to an unstable physical system poised to make a phase transition, as when a supersaturated solution is about to crystallize. In such a system, a very small impetus—the introduction of a few seed crystals, for example—can cause the phase transition to occur.

It may sound paradoxical to say that the changes which are occurring in our society are part of a cosmic pattern (and hence presumably inevitable), and at the same time that we should help them on their way by practising TM. And so, of course, it is; we have here the free will paradox on a much larger scale. Paradox is at the very heart of the cosmos. Maharishi's achievement is to show us a practical way in which this truth can be lived—in which we can experience that the thrust of life is towards ever greater freedom and expansion, and yet that to exist at all we have to conform to the laws of the universe. In Maharishi's own words:

> Since there is a way to direct the life-stream of an individual to the plane of cosmic law, the entire process of maintaining individual life and its progress and evolution can be carried on naturally and automatically. Since there is a way to regulate one's life by the laws of nature, then all one's thought, speech and action can produce an influence in accordance with these laws working for the maintenance and evolution of all things.[17]

Notes and References

Notes and References

Where details of published works appear in the Bibliography these will, for the sake of brevity, be omitted in the Notes, reference being only to the author, date and page.

Chapter One.
1. Needham, J., 1956, pp. 89–98.
2. Huxley, 1958, p. 9.
3. Ibid., p. 9.
4. Beloff, J., 1973, pp. 41–9.
5. Harlow, H. F., "Mice, Monkeys, Men and Motives"; in Bindra, D., and Stewart, J., 1971, p. 15.

Chapter Two.
1. Maharishi Mahesh Yogi, (a) 1967, p. 350.
2. Evans-Wentz, W. Y., 1954, p. 220.
3. Hudleston, Dom R., 1935, *passim*, and esp. pp. 175–6, 178.
4. Maharishi Mahesh Yogi, 1967, (a), p. 350.
5. Maharishi Mahesh Yogi, 1967, (b), p. 37.
6. Maharishi Mahesh Yogi, 1967 (a), V, 18.
7. Ibid., V, 18, Commentary.
8. Ibid., VI, 30, Commentary.

Chapter Three.
1. Dr Pugh has recorded his experience with Man Bahadur in the *Journal of Applied Physiology*, 1963, 18(6), 1234.
2. David-Neel, A., 1967, pp. 216–29.
3. Hicks, Sir C. S., "Terrestrial Animals in Cold: Exploratory Studies of Primitive Man"; in Dill, D. B., 1964, p. 410.
4. Irving, L., "Terrestrial Animals in Cold: Birds and Mammals"; in ibid., p. 375.

Chapter Four.
1. The concept of the cycle of differentiation was suggested to me by K. H. Pribram's article "Reinforcement Revisited: A Structural View", in Pribram, K. H., 1969 (d), pp. 305–46.
2. My discussion of hierarchies owes much to Arthur Koestler's *The Ghost in the Machine* (*passim*, and esp. pp. 62–136).

Chapter Five.

1. A useful introduction to the brain for the general reader is *The Nervous System*, by Peter Nathan. Another good book for the general reader is *The Mind of Man*, by Nigel Calder; this is based on a survey of research work under way throughout the world, and contains many excellent illustrations and diagrams. *The Working Brain*, by A. R. Luria, is a more technical work but also useful. *Languages of the Brain*, by Karl H. Pribram, is an illuminating and most important book, which has suggested many ideas to me. However (as Pribram himself points out in his preface) the style is by no means easy and the book is not for the casual reader.

2. Koestler, A. 1970 (b), pp. 316–36; see also MacLean, P. D., "The Paranoid Streak in Man", in Koestler, A., and Smythies, J. R., 1969.

3. Calder, N., 1970, pp. 277–8.

4. Luria, A. R., 1973, pp. 87–8.

5. Brain, Lord, and Walton, J. N., 1969, pp. 965–6.

6. Penfield, W., and Rasmussen, T., 1950, p. 235.

7. See Ornstein, R. E., 1972.

8. Needham, J., 1956, pp. 279–91.

Chapter Six.

1. Bateson, G., 1973, p. 452.

2. Miller, G. A., Galanter, E., and Pribram, K. H., 1970, *passim*, and pp. 5–19. This book seems to me a most important one, which deserves to be read not only by professional psychologists but also by novelists, theologians, physicians, and indeed everyone interested in human nature. It has the additional merit of being written most entertainingly.

3. Pribram, K. H., 1971, p. 272.

4. Ibid., pp. 312–21.

5. Ibid., pp. 320–1.

6. Livingstone, R. B., "Central Control of Receptors and Sensory Transmission Systems"; in Magoun, H. W., 1959, p. 759.

7. Wiener, N., 1961, pp. 43–4.

8. MacKay, D. M., "A Mind's Eye View of the Brain", in Pribram, K. H., 1969 (d).

Chapter Seven.

1. Levison, P. K., and Flynn, J. P., "The Objects Attacked by Cats during Stimulation of the Hypothalamus"; in Bindra, D., and Stewart, J., 1971, pp. 231–7.

2. Valenstein, E. S., Cox, V. C., and Kakolewski, J. W., "Re-examination of the Role of the Hypothalamus in Motivation"; in ibid., pp. 461–4.

3. Devor, M., Wise, R., Milgram, N. W., and Hoebel, B. G., "Physiological Control of Hypothalamically Elicited Feeding and Drinking"; in ibid., p. 480.

4. See Thorpe, W. H., 1956, pp. 108–11.

5. See Ardrey, R., 1969, p. 36.

6. MacLean, P. D., "Psychosomatics"; in Magoun H. W., 1960, p. 1731.

7. Thorpe, W. H., 1965, p. 105.

8. Köhler, W., 1957, pp. 116–17.

9. Pribram, K. H., 1971, pp. 141–66.

10. Ibid., p. 371.

Chapter Eight.

1. See Watson, L., 1973, pp. 103–5.

2. Olds, J., and Milner, P., *Journal of Comparative Physiology and Psychology*, 1954, 47, 419.

3. Nathan, P., 1973, p. 141.

4. For example, Campbell, H. J., 1973.

5. Pribram, K. H., 1971, p. 180.

6. Maharishi Mahesh Yogi, 1967 (a), VI, 27, *Commentary*.

7. Penfield, W., and Rasmussen, T., 1950, pp. 164–7.

8. Luria, A. R., 1973, pp. 45–60.

9. Pribram, K. H., 1971, p. 130.

Chapter Nine.

1. Wallace, R. K., Benson, H., and Wilson, A. F., *American Journal of Physiology*, 1971, pp. 221, 795.

2. Banquet, J. P., *Electroencephalography and Clinical Neurophysiology*, 1972, 33, 454; ibid., 1973, pp. 35, 143.

3. Orme-Johnson, D., *Psychosomatic Medicine*, 1973, 35, 341.

4. Personal communication.

5. Maharishi Mahesh Yogi, 1967 (a), V, 51, *Commentary*.

6. Quoted by Needham, J., 1956, pp. 45–6.

7. Rose, J. E., Malis, L. I., and Baker, C. P., "Neural Growth in the Cerebral Cortex after Lesions Produced by Monoenergetic Deuterons"; in Pribram, K. H., 1969 (c), pp. 22–31.

8. Pribram, K. H., 1971, pp. 34–41.

9. Hartmann, E. L., 1973, p. 27.

10. Ibid., p. 28.

11. Ibid., pp. 30–1.

12. Dement, W. C., "Studies on the Function of Rapid Eye Movement (Paradoxical) Sleep in Human Subjects"; in Pribram, K. H., 1969 (a), pp. 138–81.
13. Hartmann, E. L., 1973, p. 147.
14. Ibid., p. 129.
15. Welford, A. T., "Fatigue and Monotony"; in Edholm, O. G., and Bacharach, A. L., 1965, p. 451.
16. Hartmann, E. L., 1973, p. 77.

Chapter Ten.
1. Laski, M., 1961, p. 319.
2. Ibid., p. 280.
3. Wallas, G., *The Art of Thought*; in Vernon, P. E., 1970, pp. 91–7.
4. Lucas, F. L., 1964, p. 238.
5. Harlow, H. F., "Mice, Monkeys, Men and Motives"; in Bindra, D., and Stewart, J., 1971, pp. 112–13.
6. Lawick, Jane Goodall van-, 1971, pp. 58–9.
7. Richards, I. A., 1925, pp. 196–7.
8. Russell, B., 1967, p. 143.
9. Russell, B., 1956, p. 16.
10. Quoted by Koestler, A., 1970 (a), p. 171.
11. See De Bono, E., 1967.
12. Poincaré, H., "Mathematical Creation"; in Vernon, P. E., 1970, p. 85.
13. Ibid., pp. 83–4.
14. Hayek, F., "The Primacy of the Abstract"; in Koestler, A., and Smythies, J. R., 1969, p. 311.

Chapter Eleven.
1. *Times Literary Supplement*, 1 March 1974.
2. Bateson, G., 1973, pp. 178–9, 242–9.
3. Ibid., pp. 250–79.
4. Campbell, A., 1973, pp. 102–11.
5. Bateson, G., 1973, p. 277.

Chapter Twelve.
1. For this way of looking at the mind, I am indebted to Gregory Bateson, 1973, pp. 423–40.
2. Ibid., p. 436.
3. See Gauquelin, M., 1969.
4. Schrödinger, E., 1967, pp. 72–80.
5. Mora, P. T., *Nature*, 1963, pp. 199, 214.

6. Koestler, A., 1972, p. 90.
7. See Sciama, D. W., 1959, pp. 84 et seq.
8. Rawson, P., and Legeza, L., 1973, pp. 9–10
9. Quoted by Needham, 1956, p. 38.
10. Mascaró, J., 1965, p. 49.
11. Maharishi Mahesh Yogi, 1966, p. 33.
12. Quoted by Underhill, E., 1960, pp. 434–5.
13. Malcolm, N., 1967, p. 70n.
14. Waddington, C. H., 1961, p. 120.
15. Ibid., p. 121.

Chapter Thirteen.
1. Gauld, A., 1968, p. 355.
2. The change in attitudes towards the occult is well illustrated
   in Colin Wilson's *The Occult*. Lyall Watson's *Supernature* provides a large number of useful references; unfortunately, it is
   almost wholly uncritical and so is a good illustration of the
   tendency to wholesale swallowing of the paranormal which I
   discuss. For psychical research, one of the best books is C. D.
   Broad's *Lectures On Psychical Research*; Arthur Koestler's *The
   Roots Of Coincidence* also contains a useful summary.
3. Lilly, J. C., 1972, pp. 16–17.

Chapter Fourteen.
1. Needham, J., 1954, p. 231.
2. Maharishi Mahesh Yogi, 1967 (a), IV, 7–8.
3. Ibid., I, 40, *Commentary.*
4. Ibid., IV, 7, *Commentary.*
5. Ibid., IV, 2, *Commentary.*
6. Jerusalem, I, 15.
7. Quoted by Needham, J., 1956, p. 61.
8. Maharishi Mahesh Yogi, 1967 (a), V, 8.
9. Ibid., III, 27–8.
10. Ibid., V, 14, *Commentary.*
11. Maharishi Mahesh Yogi, 1967 (a), III, 26, *Commentary.*
12. Quoted by Needham, J., 1956, p. 68.
13. Maharishi Mahesh Yogi, 1967 (a), II, 54.
14. Ibid., II, 55.
15. Ibid., II, 55, *Commentary.*
16. Ibid., III, 23–4.
17. Maharishi Mahesh Yogi, 1966, p. 140.

Bibliography

Ardrey, R., *The Territorial Imperative*, Fontana, London, 1969.

Bateson, G., *Steps to an Ecology of Mind*, Paladin, London, 1973.

Beloff, J., *Psychological Sciences: A Preview of Modern Psychology*, Crosby Lockwood Staples, London, 1973.

Bindra, D., and Stewart, J., (eds.), *Motivation*, (2nd ed.), Penguin, Harmondsworth, 1971.

Brain, Lord, and Walton, J. N., *Diseases of the Nervous System* (7th ed.), Oxford University Press, 1969.

Broad, C. D., *Lectures on Psychical Research*, Routledge & Kegan Paul, London, 1962.

Calder, N., *The Mind of Man*, BBC Publications, London, 1970.

Campbell, A., *Seven States Of Consciousness*, Gollancz, London, 1973.

Campbell, H. J., *The Pleasure Areas*, Eyre Methuen, London, 1973.

David-Neel, A., *Magic and Mystery in Tibet*, Souvenir Press, London, 1967.

De Bono, E., *The Use of Lateral Thinking*, Cape, London, 1967.

Dill, D. B. (ed.), *Handbook of Physiology: Section 4, Adaptation to the Environment*, American Physiological Society, Washington D.C., 1964.

Edholm, O. G., and Bacharach, A. L. (Eds.), *The Physiology of Human Survival*, Academic Press, New York, 1965.

Evans-Wentz, W. Y., *The Tibetan Book of the Great Liberation*, Oxford University Press, 1954.

Gauld, A., *The Founders of the Society For Psychical Research*, Routledge, London, 1968.

Gauquelin, M., *The Cosmic Clocks*, Peter Owen, London, 1969.

Hadamard, J., *The Psychology of Invention in the Mathematical Field*, Princeton University Press, 1949.

Hartmann, E. L., *The Functions of Sleep*, Yale University Press, 1973.

Hudleston, Dom R., *The Spiritual Letters of Dom John Chapman* (2nd Ed.), Sheed & Ward, London, 1935.

Huxley, A., *The Perennial Philosophy*, Fontana, London, 1958.

James, W., *The Principles of Psychology*, New York, 1890.

Koestler, A., *The Act of Creation*, Pan, London, 1970 (a).

—*The Ghost in the Machine*, Pan, London, 1970 (b).

—*The Roots of Coincidence*, Hutchinson, London, 1972.

—and Smythies, J. R. (eds.), *Beyond Reductionism*, Hutchinson, London, 1969.

Köhler, W., *The Mentality of Apes*, Penguin, Harmondsworth. 1957.

Laski, M., *Ecstasy: A Study of Some Secular and Religious Experiences*, Cresset, London, 1961.

Lawick, Jane Goodall van-, *In the Shadow of Man*, Collins, London, 1971.

Lilly, J. C., *The Centre of the Cyclone*, Paladin, London, 1972.

Lucas, F., *Style*, Pan, London, 1964.

Luria, A. R., *The Working Brain*, Penguin, Harmondsworth, 1973.

Magoun, H. W. (ed.), *Handbook of Physiology: Section 1, Neurophysiology*, Vol. 1., American Physiological Association, Washington D.C., 1959.

—(ed.), ibid., Vol. 3, 1960.

Maharishi Mahesh Yogi, *The Science of Being and Art of Living*, International SRM Publications, 1966.

—*Bhagavad Gita; A New Translation and Commentary*, Chapters 1–6, International SRM Publications, 1967 (a).

—*Meditation*, International SRM Publications, 1967 (b).

Malcolm, N., *Ludwig Wittgenstein: A Memoir*. Oxford University Press, 1967.

Mascaró, J. (tr.), *The Upanishads*, Penguin, Harmondsworth, 1965.

Miller, G. A., Galanter, E., and Pribram, K. H., *Plans and the Structure of Behaviour*, Holt, London, New York, Sydney and Toronto, 1970.

Monod, J., *Chance and Necessity*, Collins, London, 1972.

Monroe, R. A., *Journeys out of the Body*, Corgi, London, 1974.

Nathan, P., *The Nervous System*, Penguin, Harmondsworth, 1973.

Needham, J., *Science and Civilization in China*, Vol. 1., Cambridge University Press, 1954.

—ibid., Vol. 2, 1956.

Ornstein, R. E., *The Psychology of Consciousness*, Freeman, San Francisco, 1972.

Penfield, W., and Rasmussen, T., *The Cerebral Cortex of Man*, Macmillan, New York, 1950.

Pribram, K. H., (ed.), *Brain and Behaviour 1: Mood, States and Mind*, Penguin, Harmondsworth, 1969 (a).

—(ed.), *Brain and Behaviour 2: Perception and Action*, Penguin, Harmondsworth, 1969 (b).

—(ed.), *Brain and Behaviour 3: Memory Mechanisms*, Penguin, Harmondsworth, 1969 (c).

—(ed.), *Brain and Behaviour 4: Adaptation*, Penguin, Harmondsworth, 1969 (d).

—*Languages of the Brain*, Prentice-Hall, New Jersey, 1971.

—(See Miller, G. A., Galanter, E., and Pribram, K. H.).

Rawson, P., and Legeza, L., *Tao: The Chinese Philosophy of Time and Change*, Thames and Hudson, London, 1973.

Richards, I. A., *Principles of Literary Criticism*, London and New York, 1925.

Russell, B., *Portraits from Memory*, Allen & Unwin, London, 1956.

—*Why I Am Not a Christian*, Allen & Unwin, London, 1967.

Sciama, D. W., *The Unity of the Universe*, London, 1959.

Schrödinger, E., *What is Life? and Mind and Matter*, Cambridge University Press, 1967.

Tart, C. T., *Altered States of Consciousness*, Wiley, New York, 1969.

Taylor, J., *Black Holes*, Fontana, London, 1974.

Thorpe, W. H., *Learning and Instinct in Animals*, Methuen, London, 1956.

—*Science, Man and Morals*, Methuen, London, 1965.

Underhill, E., *Mysticism* (12th ed.), Methuen, London, 1960.

Vernon, P. E., (ed.), *Creativity*, Penguin, Harmondsworth, 1970.

Waddington, C. H., *The Nature of Life*, Allen & Unwin, London, 1961.

Watson, L., *Supernature*, Hodder & Stoughton, London, 1973.

Wiener, N., *Cybernetics* (2nd Ed.), MIT Press, 1961.

Wilson, C., *The Occult*, Hodder & Stoughton, London, 1971.

Useful Addresses

Transcendental Meditation is taught in most countries through-out the world. The main national centres, from which further information can be obtained, are as follows:

GREAT BRITAIN
The Spiritual Regeneration Movement Foundation of Great Britain,
32 Cranbourn Street,
London WC2H 7EY.

USA
Students' International Meditation Society,
1015 Gayley Avenue,
Los Angeles,
California 90024.

AUSTRALIA
IMS/SIMS,
107 Jersey Road,
Woollahra,
Sydney,
New South Wales 2025.

CANADA
IMS/SIMS,
Administrative Offices for Canada,
65 Bank Street,
Ottawa,
Ontario.

NEW ZEALAND
SRM,
233 The Terrace,
Wellington.

SOUTH AFRICA
IMS South Africa,
4 Pear Tree House,
Dean Street,
Newlands,
Cape Town.

INDIA
The Spiritual Regeneration Movement Foundation of India,
The Academy of Meditation,
Shankaracharya Nagar,
Rishikesh U.P.

Index

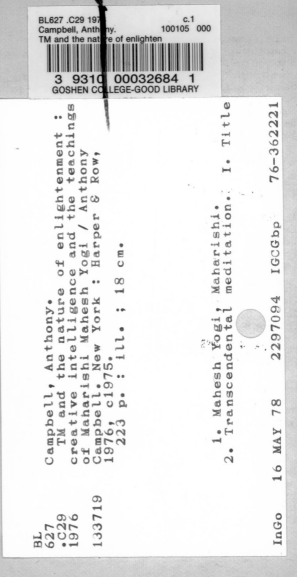